Snakecharming For Idiots

This one's for the Golden Child. Fae Iris Paterson. I know you can't read yet but just think of all the fun you're going to have when we start doing the bedtime story thing...

Making Plans for Nigel

A Beginner's Guide to Farage and UKIP

Harry Paterson

Five Leaves Publications

Making Plans for Nigel
by Harry Paterson

Published in 2015
by Five Leaves Publications,
14a Long Row, Nottingham NG1 2DH
www.fiveleaves.co.uk
www.fiveleavesbookshop.co.uk

ISBN: 978-1910170199

Designed and typeset by
Four Sheets Design and Print
Printed in Great Britain

CONTENTS

Introduction

The 2015 General Election is shaping up to be the most wide-open and closely-contested electoral battle for decades. The Conservative-led coalition is among the most unpopular of administrations in living memory, if not ever. Quite a feat, one might feel, when set next to Thatcher's epoch-defining three-term tenure that changed the face of modern Britain and so sharply divided its communities.

The Blair counter-revolution saw Labour ditch even lip-service to its historic socialist values and shamelessly ape the Tories. Today, while Miliband putters haplessly around the margins of Labour's centre-right orientation, increasing numbers of the Party's traditional voters see little difference between Cameron's genuine article and Miliband's I-can't-believe-they're-not-Tories pale-blue imitation.

Given the wide-spread unpopularity of the current Government one might reasonably have expected Labour to have enjoyed a runaway lead in the polls. That it hasn't is due to its singular failure to offer a substantive radical alternative to Conservative austerity. With the Party on record as committed to sticking to Tory spending plans there is little room for any such alternative anyway. Even if Labour was prepared to offer one. Which it clearly is not.

As late as November 2014, pollsters YouGov had Ed Miliband's personal approval ratings at an all-time low of −55. Humiliatingly, even lower than Nick Clegg's. It took Labour until 21st December 2014 to stage a mini-comeback when Opinium, in a poll conducted for the *Observer*, saw the Tories fall to twenty-nine percent with Labour on thirty-six percent. By January 2015, that lead had collapsed leaving Labour just 1.5% in front of the Conservatives. Less than a month later the Tories were back in front by a whopping six points. A month, then, is as short as a day in politics.

Further complicating matters is the fall-out from the Scottish independence referendum. Labour alienated swathes of its Scottish heartlands by siding with the Tories to save the Union. For years the SNP successfully outflanked Labour from the left — or at least appeared to — skilfully presenting itself as the party of social justice and the champion of the sort of traditional soft-left social democracy that was once Labour's uncontested home turf.

That Labour's myopia — an inevitable outcome of its detachment from its core constituency in favour of courting middle England and marching to the right — has brought the Party to the brink of extinction in Scotland is something the Party's high command fails to understand. In reality the drive for Scottish independence came not from the nationalist right but from the working class left. Voters disgusted by the twin horrors of the Conservative class offensive and Labour's capitulation to it flocked to the SNP as Alex Salmond positioned the SNP as the saviour of the Scottish working class. Only independence could save the country from further Tory ruination was the message. Despite the post-referendum triumphalism of the Unionist bloc — containing more than just a whiff of relief — the SNP came close to pulling off the biggest constitutional shake-up for centuries. Even the formally neutral monarch was forced to intervene to stave off the break-up of the British state.

The post-referendum political landscape is now a fascinating vista of seemingly limitless possible electoral outcomes. The Green Party, ignored by the mainstream media, could enter into agreement with the SNP and Plaid Cymru and might feasibly form a third-force in UK politics and condemn the Lib Dems to fourth party status. All the while "holding Labour's feet to the fire", in the words of Alex Salmond, should Labour form a minority government. Such could be the coalition of new political alliances on the parliamentary left. But what of the right?

Bizarrely, given that Cameron's government is probably the most extreme right manifestation of British Toryism yet to blight the nation, the Prime Minister is under fire from even more extreme and disaffected elements of his own Party. Despite an unashamedly ideological, anti-working class crusade — parts of which would have made even Thatcher gasp — Tory rebels from the Party's hard-right are demanding still further measures to neutralise the nascent threat of a new political phenomenon: UKIP. UKIP, however, in a string of by-elections, has shown that it poses a threat not just to the Conservatives but to Labour's share of the vote as well.

It's easy to write-off UKIP's success as the result of support from racists, bigots and xenophobes, and while such elements undoubtedly constitute the core element of both the Party's members and voters, they are only part of the reason.

Parts of the electorate — probably a majority — are sick of the greed, corruption and absence of scruple of the Westminster establishment and that of their chums in the banks and the City. Many have responded to Nigel Farage's astonishing claim that UKIP is *the* anti-establishment party, that only UKIP can offer radical change and cleanse Westminster's Augean stables. By offering himself as the People's Champion, with his amiable ordinary bloke down the pub persona, Nigel Farage has convinced a significant number of people that only he and UKIP offer a break with the sleaze and self-interest of the "Westminster elite." In so doing Farage has pulled the British body politic still further to the right. With the traditional ideological differences between Labour and Conservative submerged beneath a neo-liberal consensus, there is precious little terrain left over which to fight. As Nigel Farage put it to UKIP's 2006 Conference, "We've got three social democratic parties in

Britain — Labour, Lib Dem and Conservative are virtually indistinguishable from each other on nearly all the main issues" and "you can't put a cigarette paper between them and that is why there are nine million people who don't vote now in general elections that did back in 1992."

That all of the aforementioned has little to do with social democracy and is, in fact, determinedly neo-liberal and that there is barely a cigarette paper's difference between UKIP and the Tories' backwoodsman tendency are things that, mystifyingly, seem to escape many of Farage's working class supporters. Thus Cameron's beleaguered Tories and Miliband's shameless me-too Labour find themselves increasingly reduced to trying to out-UKIP UKIP.

Immigration hogs the lion's share of political discourse in the UK. Aided by a media obsessed with immigrants, 'illegal' aliens and refugees, Nigel Farage has coated the obsession with these topics with what many perceive to be a veneer of common sense and a blunt disdain for so-called political correctness.

In one sense, there is nothing new at all about Farage's *modus operandi*. In times of hardship and economic turmoil, the scapegoating of immigrants, foreigners and the 'othering' of minorities is a time-honoured device of populist right wing demagogues. To be fair to Farage, he's only capitalising on terrain already carefully prepared by both the Tories and Labour alike, egged on by enthusiastic cheerleaders at the *Daily Mail, The Sun, Express et al.*

A political party with only two MPs is now virtually dictating the flow of political travel in today's Britain. So how did a millionaire, pubic school-educated, former City trader-turned-politician convince the nation that only he could deal with the corruption and decadence of an establishment cabal comprising millionaires, public school-educated City traders and politicians? Why does Farage have such an appeal for so many people? How can sections of an electorate, comprising former miners, trade unionists and the natural enemies of British Conservatism support a man who once proudly boasted, "I'm the only politician keeping the flame of Thatcherism alive"?

If you have bought this book on publication the next general election will be barely a month away. This handy guide to Nigel Farage and UKIP is intended to help the undecided voter — and maybe the decided ones, too — make an informed choice when the time comes to put that cross in the little box. Given the increasing numbers of voters shunning the voting booths — in much the same way as Michael MacIntyre studiously eschews anything remotely funny in his routines — and are of the opinion that it doesn't matter for whom one votes since the government always gets in, it appears likely that future administrations will be elected by fewer and fewer people. All the more reason, then, for those potential UKIP voters to have at least a basic understanding of what they might end up with. This book looks in detail at Nigel Farage, UKIP and the party's policies. It examines Farage's anti-establishment rhetoric and compares that with his party's policies and with his and his colleagues' public pronouncements. It is a timely book because the prospect of a Tory minority government propped up by a clutch of newly-minted UKIP MPs cannot be ruled out.

Farage, a kind of Jeremy Clarkson of British politics, and his gaffe-prone colleagues, much given to jaw-dropping utterances regarding "sluts" and "Bongo Bongo Land" might well constitute a bizarre type of Prince Philip tribute act but the joke has worn very thin. They are no longer a laughing matter. While at the leadership level UKIP comprises an assortment of failed Tories, renegades and grubby chancers of the calibre of Neil and Christine Hamilton, it also continues to attract the support of working class people. Together, Farage's populist rebels could yet have a still greater impact on British politics. Not bad for a party only twenty-two years old and which was sneeringly dismissed by David Cameron, somewhat hypocritically it has to be said, as "a bunch of fruitcakes, loonies and closet racists."

This is why the Conservatives and Labour are both devoting a disproportionate amount of their time and energy to countering UKIP. This is why party leaders are desperately attempting to out-Farage Farage.

Everyone's making plans for Nigel.

Chapter 1:
Send in the Clowns

"Why does anyone have time for this creature?
He's a dim-witted racist."
UKIP founder, **Alan Sked** on Nigel Farage

Stephen Fry is reported to have once advised Neil Kinnock to drop the righteous anger the former Labour leader used to direct at Margaret Thatcher. Fry, apparently, felt it was counterproductive in that it sent a message that Thatcher was to be considered a serious opponent and that those expressions of anger only exposed Kinnock's weaknesses, where the late Prime Minister was concerned. Far better to laugh at her; make her a figure of fun and reduce her in the public's eye, advised Fry. It was advice that the intemperate Kinnock chose to ignore so we'll never know how effective such a strategy might have been. In today's climate, however, it seems, at best, unlikely to be successful and, at worst, to be positively dangerous.

Take Boris Johnson, for example. How can you effectively mock a man who sends himself up as skilfully as he does? As someone who has craftily played the Boris the Buffoon card for all its worth he has ensured that any attempts at ridiculing him have already been neutered. Many a Labour voter was happy to cast a vote for Johnson as London Mayor as he was perceived as a 'bit of a laugh.' As someone whose slips, gaffes and self-deprecating observations made him far more human than the grey, humourless bureaucrats one normally associates with the professional politician.

His appearances on *Have I Got News For You* reveal a politician whose people skills enabled him to make even a derisory inability to read an autocue an object of endearment and to win people over to laugh along *with* him, rather than *at* him. The fact is, however, that the oafish, bumbling, amiable toff persona masks a shrewd intelligence and finely-honed class instincts.

For many people, their first real conscious awareness of UKIP will have been as a result of one its members' somewhat less than considered public utterances. There have been many and while comedy isn't something that people automatically associate with politics UKIP has certainly induced at least one smirk or chuckle for every expression of outrage its members provoke.

It might well be stretching things to credit Nigel Farage with quite the same degree of guile as Boris Johnson but it's inarguable that for most of his career the UKIP leader appears to have been coated with Teflon, rather than mortal skin. As well as with his own indiscretions, Farage has proved adept at spinning his party members' outrageous proclamations as things at which to be amused; matters not to be taken seriously and as episodes at which we can all have a giggle. What a refreshing contrast to the cynical, coached-to-death fakes of the 'Westminster elite.' How much more human such people are when compared to the cowardly PC brigade, afraid to speak their minds when a shot of good old fashioned British common sense is needed. This is the message Farage adroitly peddles. And it takes no mean skill, considering the nature of some of those utterances...

"Since the passage of the Marriage (Same Sex Couples) Act, the nation has been beset by serious storms and floods. One recent one caused the worst flooding for sixty years. The Christmas floods were the worst for 127 years. Is this just global warming or is there something more serious at work?"

DAVID SILVESTER

"As for the links between homosexuality and paedophilia, there is so much evidence that even a full-length book could hardly do justice to the subject." DR JULIA GASPER

"The evidence is quite clear that the percentage of homosexuals who molest children is very high and cannot be dismissed." JAN ZOLYNIAK

"I just wish they would keep their homosexual nature and practices to themselves and stop trying to ram it down my throat telling me they are 'normal' when they are not."

DOUGLAS DENNY

"If you look at the people who get degrees more, women get them and they are getting the jobs in the workplace but for various reasons they don't have the ambition to go right to the top because something gets in the way. It's called a baby." STUART AGNEW

"Compulsory abortion when the foetus is detected as having Down's, spina bifida or similar syndrome which, if it is born, could render the child a burden on the state as well as on the family." GEOFFREY CLARK

"Above all, one should not shy away of contemplating forced repatriation, or threatening it to further assimilation, as a result of their [Muslims] lack of economic contribution to the UK." Abhijit Pandya

More recently, on January 8th, 2015 Heather Saul wrote in *The Independent*:

A UKIP councillor was allegedly expelled from the party for saying she had a problem with black people because there was "something about their faces," it has been reported.

15

Rozanne Duncan was forced to leave UKIP for "bringing the party into disrepute" reportedly in "jaw-dropping" remarks made to a BBC documentary-maker during filming for a programme about UKIP in South Thanet, but exactly what she said was not revealed at the time. Now, The Times reports that an account provided to UKIP quoted her as allegedly saying she had a "problem" with black people, who she called "negroes". Ms Duncan then allegedly insisted she was "not racist" because she had "many Asian shopkeeper and local business friends".

Previously a Conservative, Ms Duncan was elected in her constituency after a by-election in May 2013.The 68-year-old, who now represents Cliftonville East ward on Thanet district council as an independent, was given 28 days to appeal UKIP decision.

Ms Duncan, who has not responded to requests for a comment from The Independent, apparently refused to confirm or deny to The Times that she had made the reported comments. According to the paper, she claimed to have been treated "very badly" by UKIP and she also claimed her remarks had not been conveyed to the party in context.

All of these are merely snapshots of seemingly typical UKIP thinking. And we haven't even mentioned Godfrey Bloom yet.

It is no exaggeration to say that this book could be filled solely with reports of such incidents involving UKIP members. And yet Farage and his party appear to have sustained remarkably little damage.

There is also the baffling amount of media coverage Farage and UKIP receive, accompanied by an even more mystifying lack of real depth and tough questioning on the part of his media interrogators. Between 2009 and 2013, Farage appeared more times on the BBC's flagship current affairs programme, Question Time, than any other guest. A bizarre state of affairs for a party leader who, during that period, didn't have a single MP.

Online and print media have been equally generous, to the frustration of the Green Party which, until late 2014, had been virtually ignored despite having one MP and control of Brighton and Hove Council since 2010. UKIP would take a further three years before it won a majority of seats on any council in the UK.

An amusingly satirical take in *The Huffington Post* on May 23rd 2014 made the point perfectly. Headed, Local Council Election Results: UKIP Gains Control Of Large Sections Of The Media, the piece read:

> Britain woke up today to find that UKIP had made huge gains across the country's media. UKIP won seats in news studios all over England and Wales, including taking total control of airtime in London. The previously safe Tory area of the BBC also saw a huge swing to the party. "It's a remarkable victory for Nigel Farage's party, especially considering that they don't run a single council," said one pundit. "Clearly, Britain has lost overall control of UKIP."

The media seems obsessed with UKIP but at the same time the party is strangely exempt from the sort of rigorous and gruelling questioning and examination to which all the other parties are subjected. When one considers the absence of any kind of manifesto the situation becomes even more farcical. With just weeks left until the 2015 General Election, UKIP's manifesto simply doesn't exist. As John Grace noted in the *Guardian* on January 21st, 2015,

> In 2010 UKIP laid out its policies in a 486-page manifesto compiled by a few delinquent party activists. Its proposals included introducing a dress code for taxi drivers, repainting trains in traditional colours, insisting on a proper dress code for theatre-goers, making the Circle line on London's tube circular again, scrapping maternity leave, investigating racism against white people at the BBC, teaching schoolchildren about the roles of Arab and African countries in promoting slavery, and reintroducing capital punishment. Four years later, Nigel Farage admitted that the manifesto had basically been a load of nonsense and that he had never read it.
>
> Just six weeks before their new manifesto is due to be launched, Tim Aker has either quit his post as Ukip's head of policy or been sacked. Ukip insists the manifesto is still fully on track; if so, Aker is the only person who knows what is in it, and is keeping it a secret. No one else in the party apparently has

a clue. With two sitting MPs and more hoped for in May, it is proving a great deal harder than expected for Ukip to come up with something credible, fully costed and which everyone can support. Douglas Carswell, Mark Reckless and Farage find it hard enough to agree on anything as it is: coming up with something that will appeal both to the neolibertarians and the former BNP members who make up its grassroots is a near impossibility.

As the *Guardian's* Rowena Mason explained the day before,

Ukip has replaced its policy chief, who is in charge of writing the party's manifesto, with less than four months to go before the general election.

Tim Aker, an MEP and parliamentary candidate for the key marginal of Thurrock, has stepped down to concentrate on his campaigning, and has been replaced by the deputy chair, Suzanne Evans.

There is a battle within Ukip between those who want to modernise the party and others, who want it to stick to its core values.

There have been worries about whether the manifesto will be ready for the party's spring conference at the end of February.

It is intended to be a fully costed, mature, policy document that shows Ukip has grown up as a party since its 2010 manifesto — which included pledges to make the circle line on London's underground circular again and to enforce a proper dress code at the theatre [yes, seriously].

A party spokesman stressed Aker had not been sacked but decided to stand down. The MEP tweeted: "Delighted to have handed over strong policy brief to the excellent @Suzanne Evans1. Now on to winning #Thurrock in May!"

Evans said Aker was "extremely bright" and had done an excellent job on Ukip policy, adding that it was only his MEP commitments that meant he could not continue.

It isn't an exaggeration to say that such a state of affairs is unprecedented in British politics. Despite the enormous teams of specialists and experts, encompassing every area of policy, which put together the manifestos for the Conservatives, Labour and Liberal Democrats, their leaders and representatives can expect to be relentlessly interrogated regarding their manifestos. UKIP, by contrast, don't even *have* a manifesto and yet is given what amounts to a comparatively free ride.

These are all serious matters and yet it is hard to dissociate UKIP from the sheer comedic spectacle of its members and representatives, as typified by the aforementioned, attempting to convince the electorate that it is a credible political force, deserving of being taken seriously. Something comedy character The Pub Landlord, as realised by comedian Al Murray, seems to understand. If UKIP can be said to be a Prince Philip tribute act then what are we to make of Murray's latest comedic venture? Has UKIP inspired its very own tribute act? A tribute of a tribute, you might say?

Murray has launched his Free United Kingdom Party (FUKP) and is busily campaigning in Kent in a bid to enter parliament. Among his recent contributions to contemporary political debate are such gems of political perception that the country needs "... a bloke waving a pint offering common-sense solutions." That under FUKP we'd be "out of Europe by 2025, out of the Solar System by 2050." Displaying a marvellously Faragian populist touch he also commits a FUKP government to lowering the price of beer to a penny a pint, bricking up the Channel Tunnel and deploying Spitfire squadrons to patrol the coast to keep out those bloody foreigners. Murray brims with confidence and good cheer on the campaign trail but worries that Farage might steal FUKP's obviously "common sense policies."

Before we can really understand Nigel and UKIP today, though, we need to understand where the party came from. For that you can thank Alan Sked, the party's creator. Currently Professor of International History at the London School of Economics (LSE), Sked is a decades-long committed Eurosceptic and political activist. Over the course of his unusual political trajectory the Prof has stood as a Liberal candidate, eventually falling out with them over Europe, natch, before stints with the Anti-Federalist League, UKIP's predecessor, which he also founded, and then, of course, UKIP itself.

Sked's ten years as Convenor of European Studies, one of the LSE's postgraduate MA programmes seems to have inculcated in him a fierce opposition to the European Union. He believes it to be a corrupt, anti-democratic body which directly threatens the economic interests of the United Kingdom. Also featuring on his CV is his founding-membership of the Bruges Group.

The Group explains its aims and objectives thus:

> *The Bruges Group is an independent all-party think tank. Our independence is our strength allowing us to be free to follow our own policy agenda and put the national interest above party political considerations.*
>
> *Set up in February 1989, its aim was to promote the idea of a less centralised European structure than that emerging in Brussels. Its inspiration was Margaret Thatcher's Bruges speech in September 1988, in which she remarked that, "we have not successfully rolled back the frontiers of the state in Britain, only to see them reimposed at a European level, with a European superstate exercising a new dominance from Brussels."*
>
> *The Bruges Group has had a major effect on public opinion, and forged links with Members of Parliament as well as with similarly minded groups in other countries.*
>
> *Through its groundbreaking publications and wide-ranging discussions The Bruges Group has spearheaded the intellectual battle against the notion of ever closer union in Europe and will continue its fight against further integration and, above all, against British involvement in a single European state.*
>
> *The Group also holds regular high-profile public meetings, seminars, debates and conferences. These enable influential speakers to contribute to the European debate.*

Alas, Sked was expelled by the Group in 1991 for the sin of founding the Anti-Federalist League (AFL) a clearly-defined political party which ran its own candidates in the 1992 General Election, one of whom was Sked himself.

The following year Professor Sked contested two by-elections. The first at Newbury, where an enthusiastic Enoch Powell blessed Sked with his approval, and then at Christchurch. In both contests Sked came fourth behind the three main parties, which wasn't too shabby at all, especially at Newbury where a total of nineteen candidates stood. Reckoning he was on to something, based on those two results, Sked then changed the name of the AFL, gave it a re-boot and the United Kingdom Independence Party (UKIP) was born.

In what was starting to look suspiciously like a bit of a pattern, Sked's tenure as UKIP boss was short-lived. Just four years later he was out. Factionalism, in-fighting and the increasing influence of far-right elements prompted him to remark that UKIP was "doomed to remain on the political fringes." Whatever undoubted academic and intellectual talents the Prof has, the gift of prophecy is not among them.

Thereafter Sked turned on his creation — likened by him to a "Frankenstein's monster". In a frank interview with the *Guardian's* Stuart Jeffries, on May 26th, 2014, he claimed, "up until 1997 I managed to keep Ukip a liberal — with a small 'l' — centre, moderate party." A description of UKIP that is so far from today's incarnation of the party as to be entirely unrecognisable. Quoting from the Party's 1993 membership application form Sked went on to say that, originally, UKIP was "... a non-sectarian, non-racist party with no prejudices against foreigners or lawful minorities of any kind. It does not recognise the legitimacy of the European parliament and will send representatives only to the British parliament in Westminster. They got rid of all that after I left."

He was only just getting warmed up, however. "They took out the bit about no prejudices against lawful minorities and, as soon as I disappeared, they all decided they wanted to go to the European parliament and take their expenses." Jeffries queried that such changes didn't automatically make UKIP a racist party, surely? "The *de facto* leader of Ukip [Farage] since 1999 has been a racist political failure," Sked insisted firmly before telling Jeffries, "He wanted ex-National Front candidates to run and I said, 'I'm not sure about that,' and he said, 'There's no need to worry about the nigger vote. The nig-nogs will never vote for us.' Yes, you read that correctly. Sked said, "I was shocked. I had never heard people use those words. At the time, others thought he was being funny. I didn't. They showed what kind of man he is."

Farage has always denied saying such a thing. However when challenged by Sked to sue him for slander and libel the current UKIP chief has, so far, declined to accept the challenge. Sked continued, "If he runs in South Thanet, his agent will be a man called Martyn Heale who was a National Front organiser in west London." Far-right trainspotters will know Martyn Heale, the National Front's Hammersmith Branch boss before ending up in UKIP where he became Nigel Farage's election agent in 2005. Heale was apparently banned from joining UKIP until Sked quit.

"The party I founded has become a Frankenstein's monster," Sked told Jeffries. "When I was leader, we wouldn't send MEPs to Europe because we didn't want to legitimise it. My policy was that if we were forced to take the salaries, we would give them to the National Health Service — they wouldn't be taken by the party or individuals. Now Ukip say they're against welfare cheats coming from eastern Europe, but in fact *they're* the welfare cheats. They do nothing in the European parliament and take the money. They're no better than these people on [Channel 4 documentary series] Benefits Street. Farage has become a millionaire from expenses. There's no reason to vote for UKIP because if they believed in what they said they wouldn't be there." On the day this book went to press an employee of the UKIP MEP, Janet Atkinson, was found to be "repatriating" money by inflating restaurant bills, causing her boss to be dropped as a candidate in the UK elections.

Jeffries' suggestion that perhaps the job of UKIP MEPs is to expose the nature of the EU and that their presence, salaries and expenses are necessary evils to facilitate that work was laughingly dismissed by Sked. "Oh, that's nonsense! They're hardly ever there. They just turn up for expenses. They don't turn up for the key debates." It appears that on those rare occasions when UKIP MEPs do turn up, they don't have much idea what they should be doing anyway. "When there were only three UKIP MEPs, the LSE European Studies Institute found they voted three different ways," said Sked.

Commenting on UKIP's success during local and European elections, Sked continued to unload: "I feel very sorry for voters who are now going to have as councillors people who aren't very sophisticated, who have no local government policies and who have no experience in running things. All UKIP is good for, if their behaviour in Strasbourg and Brussels is anything to go by, is taking public money. If you elect a UKIP MEP, you're just going to elect another incompetent charlatan that you're going to turn into another millionaire. They go native in Brussels, take the expenses and the perks and do fuck all."

Remarking on Farage's everyman persona Sked finished with a withering *coup de grace*. "Behind that image is someone who isn't bright. I spent two hours trying to explain to him the difference between 'it's' with an apostrophe and 'its' without and he just flounced out the office saying, 'I just don't understand words.'"

Regarding letters of complaint arising from Farage's campaign in Salisbury in 1997, Sked recalled, "I remember one that said, 'I'm very glad your candidate believes in education, but until he learns to spell it, I'm not voting for him.' That's the kind of person people are voting for when they vote UKIP. Why does anyone have time for this creature? He's a dim-witted racist."

Chapter 2:
From Little Acorns

"The only people I do have problems with are negroes.
I really do have a problem with people with negroid features."
Former UKIP councillor **Rozanne Duncan**

Accusations by Sked of Farage being a racist might well be on the money and, judging the matter purely on that which emanates from Farage's mouth, it probably is, but it wouldn't be unreasonable to consider some hypocrisy on Sked's part. After all, for all his new-found small-l liberalism and multicultural inclusivity, there is the minor matter of him sharing a platform with Enoch Powell. Enoch, as most will know, wouldn't normally be considered a paragon of progressive anti-racism.

Farage's mates and acquaintances have a somewhat different take where our hero is concerned. One-time buddy Richard North reckons, "If he is a racist, then he's also a consummate actor, because he hides it that well. Personally I don't think he is. I think he's an old-fashioned jingoistic patriot." Jingoistic patriotism eh? Even the most dour-faced lefty cynic would find it a bit of a leap to imagine that such sunny-natured love of country could slide into outright racism, surely?

North was a former RAF officer and then the boss of his own consultancy before ending up in the European Parliament as a Research Director for the Eurosceptic European Democracies and Diversities Group, where he shared an office with Farage. Perhaps he has not quite the required class and political background to offer impartial and objective commentary regarding the UKIP leader. If this author might be permitted to offer a bit of advice it might be best if Nigel found other character references when next he updates his CV.

So where did it all start for Farage? He was born on April 3rd, 1964 in Downe, near Sevenoaks in Kent. His father, Guy Justus Oscar Farage, ensured Farage shared the family lineage with its Huguenot ancestors. French Protestants, in case you were wondering. A 'beautiful British name' as The Pub Landlord might be moved to observe.

One of Nigel's great grandfathers was from German immigrant stock who moved to London in the 19th century and his father was a stockbroker who worked in the City.

As befits the would-be saviour of the poor and huddled masses Farage's beginnings were humble with his education courtesy of Dulwich College. The fee-paying private school was established in 1619 by Elizabethan actor Edward Alleyn, with the original intention of educating twelve scholars as the foundation of 'God's Gift.'

The cost of an education at Dulwich College is between £17,403 per year — for non-boarding pupils — and £36,324 per year for boarders. With, probably, another £10K lumped on for kit and trips to Klosters and so on. The average UK wage is around £26,000 per year, by the way.

It seems Farage's politics were pretty well established by the time he was just sixteen, while at Dulwich. On September 19th, 2013, Michael Crick, for *Channel 4 News,* shared some interesting findings. Crick claimed that during Farage's time at the prestigious school, in the late 70s and early 80s, evidence had been uncovered by Channel 4 which suggested Farage's teachers considered him a "racist", "fascist" and/or "neo-fascist."

Channel 4 had turned up a lengthy letter, dated June 1981 by one of Dulwich's then English teachers, Chloe Deakin. In the letter Deakin pleads with the Head, David Emms, to rethink his appointment of Farage as a prefect.

Among other observations there is one remark by a fellow teacher who considered that should Farage be "a fascist" it shouldn't necessarily prevent the future politician from making a perfectly good prefect. The letter records that this observation prompted "considerable reaction" from other members of staff. The letter continued: "Another colleague, who teaches the boy, described his publicly professed racist and neo-fascist views; and he cited a particular incident in which Farage was so offensive to a boy in his set, that he had to be removed from the lesson. This master stated his view that this behaviour was precisely why the boy should not be made a prefect. Yet another colleague described how, at a Combined Cadet Force (CCF) camp organised by the college, Farage and others had marched through a quiet Sussex village very late at night shouting Hitler-youth songs.

Farage has claimed in *Fighting Bull*, one of his three memoirs, that the controversy regarding his prefecture was because of his admiration of and affinity for Enoch Powell but as Crick noted for Channel 4, Chloe Deakin's letter suggests Farage would more accurately have been located well to the right of Powell.

It seems Farage was considered by some staff to be rude, cheeky and disruptive with a fondness for winding-up those teachers he considered to be left wing. When questioned by Crick he was dismissive of any suggestion he had been sympathetic to the fascist cause. "I did say things that would offend deeply and there were certainly two or three members of the English staff I made arguments against that I didn't necessarily believe in. But any accusation I was ever involved in far right politics is utterly untrue."

Farage's response to Crick's questioning regarding the singing of Hitler Youth songs was emphatic: "That's silly. I don't know any Hitler youth songs, in English or German. Of course I said some ridiculous things, not necessarily racist things. It depends how you define it. You've got to remember that ever since 1968 up until the last couple of years, we've not been able in this country, intelligently to discuss immigration, to discuss integration, it's all been a buried subject and that's happened through academia, it's happened through politics and the media."

While there are former Dulwich staff and pupils who have memories of Farage as a fascist there are others who see his youthful outbursts as no more than the ill-judged excesses of youth. Others recall his politics being more akin to Thatcherism. Whatever the truth of the matter, it's apparent that Farage's core politics are long-standing. He has what we might term *form*.

Nigel's mum, though, maintains her son was a good scholar and that his final school report included the observation that his *alma mater* "... would be a poorer place without this boy's personality".

After distinguishing himself at Dulwich, Farage took the unusual step of leaving to go straight to work, rather than to university. Following his father into the City, he joined US commodities brokers Drexel Burnham Lambert at the London Metal Exchange. He followed this with stints at Credit Lyonnais Rouse in 1986 until 1994 when he joined Refco before moving again to Natexis Metals in 2003.

It was in the City that Farage first met his close friend Steven Spencer who recalled their first encounter: "My first impression of Nigel is unorthodox, a happy, cheerful guy, outspoken and humorous." Speaking to BBC Radio 4 in December, 2012, Spencer continued, "When I worked as a customer of Nigel's I would wander into a smoke-filled room, with tobacco smoke about 4 feet from the floor, with a bunch of very happy traders and good chemistry around Nigel." The reader will be astonished to learn that, according to Spencer, "There'd always be a very politically incorrect atmosphere that just relaxed everybody."

Farage lives "around the corner from his mother" and has been married twice. First in 1988 to Gráinne Hayes, with whom he had two children; Samuel (born 1989) and Thomas (born 1991). They divorced in 1997. In 1999 he married Kirsten Mehr, a German national, with whom he had two more children, Victoria (born 2000) and Isabelle (born 2005).

Kirsten is employed by Farage as his parliamentary secretary which has drawn accusations of milking the system given that her wages are paid by tax payers. In response to the criticism, which given Farage's anti-immigrant and anti-European stances — not to mention his condemnation of the 'Westminster elite' and their expenses-fiddling proclivities — might leave him exposed as a hypocrite, he asserts that of Europe's 742.5 million inhabitants, only the — clearly uniquely gifted — Mrs. Farage is capable of doing the job.

A Tory since his school days, Farage left the Conservative Party in 1993 in protest at then Prime Minister John Major's signing of the Maastricht Treaty and co-founded UKIP with Sked, among others.

Initially, UKIP's central *raison d'être* was purely to secure the UK's withdrawal from the EU. Virtually a single-issue party, it became a pole of attraction for Eurosceptic Tories who, under John Major's premiership, came to the fore when the Conservative Party found itself riven across Euro lines when sterling was forced from the European Exchange Rate Mechanism (ERM) in 1992.

Disillusioned Tories were bolstered by an influx from the far-right and assorted Nazis from the National Front, BNP and others who found UKIP a potentially more successful platform than their previous outfits. In 1997 the party fielded several candidates in that year's general election who were forced to watch their thunder stolen by James Goldsmith's Referendum Party which fought nearly 550 seats. In the 165 constituencies where both UKIP and the Referendum Party stood, UKIP were beaten by Goldsmith's candidates in 163.

Sked condemned his party as something "... infected by the far-right" but mistakenly predicted it was "doomed to remain on the political fringes." The collapse of the Referendum Party, following Goldsmith's death, ensured UKIP would survive by mopping up its members.

In 1999, following a successful leadership challenge by millionaire businessman, Michael Holmes, UKIP won three seats in that year's elections to the European Parliament with its 7% share of the vote. Holmes himself secured a win in the South West England constituency with Jeffrey Titford taking East of England and Nigel Farage triumphing in the South East England seat. Our hero was on his way.

But first there was the unedifying spectacle of a power-struggle at the top of the party. Holmes infuriated many party members by calling for more powers for the European Parliament. A somewhat unconventional stance for an anti-EU politician leading an avowedly Eurosceptic party. Unable to withstand the wrath of the rank-and-file Holmes, along with the entire National Executive Committee, was forced to resign. He tried to continue as an independent MEP but lost the resulting legal battle and was then replaced by Graham Booth, the second listed UKIP candidate on the South West England ballot paper.

In the 2001 general election UKIP fielded over 420 candidates but gained only 1.5% of the vote and won no Westminster seats. Despite both the Welsh Assembly and the Scottish Parliament using proportional representation, rather than Westminster's first past the post system, both Scotland and Wales declined to elect any UKIP candidates. After the general election, Titford, who'd been party leader since Holmes' exit in 2000, resigned as boss but stayed as an elected MEP. He was succeeded by Roger Knapman.

While Farage's enemies can easily level charges of hypocrisy against him, given his membership of the European Parliament, even his friends find his position odd, with Steven Spencer telling BBC Radio 4 that "We always joked with him about that — if you dislike it so much, what are you doing there? But Nigel's view has always been, to me, that the place to change it is inside, not outside." Nigel Farage claims that he is anti-EU, not necessarily anti-Europe, as if that somehow squares his inconsistent circle. As he is fond of pointing out, again somewhat bizarrely thinking the point proves his case rather than demolishing it, his wife, and Parliamentary Secretary, is German.

Farage does have European allies and admirers. Timo Soini, leader of the far right Fins Party, says "He's very outspoken — even the people who don't share his message think that he's a great speaker and fun to listen to." He continues admiringly, "Nigel is so quick and so intelligent that it's very hard to beat him, but the real political elite in Europe, they would rather have parliament without Mr Farage."

There is no doubt that Farage is a witty and talented public speaker, with many of his set-piece speeches garnering plaudits from even those naturally opposed to his politics. A rapier-like cruelty is often to be found among the humorous asides as former President of the European Council, Herman van Rompuy, discovered when Farage, snobbishly described him as "having the appearance of a low grade bank clerk" as well as possessing "... the charisma of a damp rag." This outburst resulted in an official reprimand and a fine of 3,000 Euros when the unrepentant Farage refused to apologise for his "insulting" personal attack.

Richard North ascribes Farage's larger-than-life public performances as typical of someone much less self-assured than his audience might perceive him to be. "I spent a lot of time with him — very, very close to him. Although he comes over as a very friendly, bubbly open individual, behind the scenes he's very insecure," said North, speaking to BBC Radio 4. He continued, "It is part of his charm — hard-living, hard-drinking, and hard-smoking — that is who he is and why he is able to attract a following." But "he cannot work with people in a detailed long-term relationship. What he actually does is that he uses people and he uses them up — he consumes people. When you actually look at his career and his progress, it's a succession of teams around him. People join him, they get enthused by him, and then see the inner Farage, become disillusioned and then peel off — rather like me, but there are hundreds of me, in that sense. But if you're looking for a serious politician, with a strategic brain, who is able to lead a party and develop and expand a party, well, they're not the same people. Perhaps UKIP's tragedy is it has this tremendously effective figurehead, but it has no strategic brain."

Farage's close friends have a more nuanced take on the mercurial politician. Former UKIP MEP Godfrey Bloom, about whom much more later, paints a picture of, if not exactly a Renaissance Man, a man who does have at least some interest in things outside politics. Albeit ones which sit perfectly with his jingoism and enthusiastic Brit-centrism. Apparently Farage is quite the fan of classic Brit sitcoms like Dad's Army and is also a cricket devotee. His greatest passion, however, is the history of World War 1 and he regularly tours the battlefields of the Great War in the company of friends, collectively known as 'Farage's Foragers.' "He's deeply interested in Europe, and the history of Europe and where it's gone wrong. He likes people to understand what Britain went through in two world wars and what our position is in Europe — he's passionately interested," added Spencer, during his Radio Four interview.

The tours, says Bloom, are often referred to as "... bottlefield Tours" which hints at the alcohol-fuelled character of the Farage-led sorties. "I remember we were in Ypres, it was about 3:00am in the morning, we must have drunk the restaurant completely dry — it was one hell of a session, and I called time. I staggered up into bed, and Farage shouted at me, 'lightweight' and that really sums him up. His lifestyle is appalling; he'd be the first to admit it. He drinks too much red wine and he smokes too much. Unless I can persuade him to slow down — and nobody else has succeeded — he won't have a future. He'll fall off his perch."

Perhaps unexpectedly, or maybe not given his anti-Muslim rhetoric, Farage describes himself as a

Christian, albeit a "somewhat lapsed" member of the Church of England, a body traditionally known as the Tory Party at prayer. Speaking to the *Telegraph's* Christina Odone, in November 2013, Farage laid out his position in typically blunt fashion: "We need a much more muscular defence of our Judaeo-Christian heritage. Yes, we're open to different cultures but we have to defend our values. That's the message I want to hear from the Archbishop of Canterbury and from our politicians. Anything less is appeasement of the worst kind." Yet Farage's position seems not to be driven by any genuinely religious commitment and far more by the politics of identity and culture. As something to be appropriated in the service of marking out clear red, white and blue lines between 'us' and 'them.' As Odone herself reflects, "... he speaks not as a defender of the faith — he ventures to church only four or five times a year — but of "our identity.""

Odone further notes, "His list of those who will have no place in a Ukip Britain also includes Muslims who speak no English and wear the veil." Farage claimed "It makes people feel deeply uncomfortable. We go on about equality but under our noses, female genital mutilation has been going on in this country. Tens of thousands of women a year, but is anyone talking about it? It's brushed under the carpet." An abhorrent practice, to be sure, but, typically, Farage offers no sources or evidence for his claims. In reality the NHS's official position — and you'd think they'd know — "... is that the true extent is unknown, due to the 'hidden' nature of the crime."

As for non-English speaking Muslims, latest figures (see below) estimate these total about 6% of all UK Muslims. A statistically insignificant number.

Nigel is resilient if nothing else and the chances that an absence of proof, evidence or anything resembling the truth might keep such a good man down are remote. His remarks on Muslim ghettos and no-go areas, in wake of the *Charlie Hebdo* murders are instructive. On January 7th Saïd and Chérif Kouachi stormed the Parisian offices of French satirical magazine *Charlie Hebdo*. The brothers were armed with a variety of automatic weapons and proceeded to kill eleven journalists and staff, injuring a further twelve.

Sensing an opportunity to push the UKIP cause, Farage told America's Fox News that most of France's larger cities contained no-go zones for Muslims. The French Embassy in London was appalled and likened his remarks to those made by so-called terrorism expert Steve Emerson who, prior to Farage's ill-advised nonsense, claimed, also on Fox News, that Birmingham was a strictly Muslims-only area.

An Embassy spokesman said, "Of course it is not true to say that there are no-go areas in France. To give you an idea of how wide of the mark those comments are, we could compare them to those by the American journalist who recently said that non-Muslims simply did not go any longer to Birmingham. In both cases those statements are obviously totally untrue. The *'marche républicaine'* on Sunday was an excellent example of the unity of the French population when facing terrorism."

Nigel was on a roll, though, and followed his initial claim by insisting that "big ghettos" had sprung up across Europe while respective governments ignored the phenomenon. Apparently the UK government ignored the operation of sharia law, female genital mutilation and the grooming and sexual abuse of children in areas such as Rochdale and Rotherham: "It isn't just France, it is happening right across Europe. We have got no-go zones across most of the big French cities. We have been turning a blind eye to preachers of hate coming here and saying things for which most of the rest of us would be arrested. In parts of northern England, we have seen the sexual grooming scandals of underage girls committed by Muslim men, in the majority, and for all of these things we have seen the law not being applied equally. We have seen the police forces not actually doing their job because we have suffered from moral cowardice. We have, through mass immigration and not checking the details of people who have come to our countries, we have allowed big ghettos to develop. When it comes to the big issues we have been led very badly."

He further claimed that "tens of thousands of young women" had suffered forced genital mutilation while resident in the UK and that "We even, a few years ago, had some quite clear examples where the immigration services were actually allowing women to come into Britain from Pakistan and elsewhere to join polygamous marriages — something that is against our law. So wherever you look, wherever you look, you see this blind eye being turned and you see the growth of ghettos where the police and all the normal agents of the law have withdrawn and that is where sharia law has come in and you know it got so bad in Britain that our last archbishop of Canterbury, the leader of our church, actually said we should accept sharia law."

Farage declined to offer proof of his inflammatory and sensationalist remarks and the specific cities in France and across Europe which hosted Muslim only "no-go zones" were not named. *Quelle surprise.*

Referring to child abuse, for a moment, one can only marvel at the irrational prejudice required to make capital from 'Muslim grooming gangs' while remaining silent about the staggering numbers of children raped by members of the white British male establishment. Margaret Thatcher's friend Jimmy Saville alone probably accounts for more instances of child abuse than those of all the so-called Muslim grooming gangs put together. Not to mention the evidence pointing to a decades-long organised conspiracy of child rape, and possibly even murder, reaching right into the very heart of the establishment, involving parliament, the police, judiciary and monarchy. Cyril Smith, anyone?

It's a common tactic of the far right everywhere, from the Islamophobic English Defence League to Le Pen's *Front National* and back to UKIP; to urge the need to 'defend' 'our' faith and culture, implying that it is under sustained attack from rampaging hoards of barbarian Muslims, intent on destroying the good old British way of life and establishing a UK-wide caliphate. But where's the evidence? How likely is such a 'threat'?

For a start the numbers simply don't support the argument that Islam poses any kind of threat to the UK. As the *Guardian* reported in October 2014, "Britons overstate the proportion of Muslims in their country by a factor of four, according to a new survey by Ipsos Mori that reveals public understanding of the numbers behind the daily news in 14 countries. People from the UK also think immigrants make up twice the proportion of the population as is really the case." Confirmation that mainstream media's virtual obsession with Islam and the constant diet of Islam-related scare stories have a real impact on the attitudes and thinking of the general population.

In reality the 2011 Census reported that Muslims accounted for 2,786,635 people; just 4.4% of the entire UK population. In February, 2015, however, new figures were released which appeared to show that the UK's Muslim population has almost doubled since 2001. Perhaps Farage and fellow Islamophobes are correct after all, then? Apparently not. Behind the headlines some interesting facts emerge. As *The Independent's* Loulla-Mae Eleftheriou-Smith explained on February 12th, 2015.

> The Muslim population in the UK has nearly doubled across England and Wales since 2001 to 2.71 million, but almost half live in the most deprived local authorities.
> Analysis of the 2011 census by the Muslim Council of Britain shows a "frank snapshot" of the state of British Muslim life, Dr Sundas Ali, an analyst for the report, said.

In 2001, 1.55 million Muslims lived in England and Wales, which grew to 2.71 million in 2011, with a further 77,000 Muslims living in Scotland and 3,800 in Ireland.

Though the 2011 data showed that only one in 20 of the UK's overall population is Muslim, 46 per cent of the Muslim population lives in the 10 per cent most deprived local authority districts in England.

Despite more than half of the UK's Muslim population having been born abroad, 73 per cent state that their only national identity is British, and only six per cent of the whole British Muslim population were found to be struggling with speaking English.

There is a higher than national average of young Muslim people in England and Wales, with 33 per cent under the age of 15, while Muslim children represented one in 12 of all school age children in 2011.

Nearly quarter of the Muslim population over that age of 16 have degree level qualifications or higher, and the total of Muslims with no qualifications dropped from 39 per cent to 26 per cent over the 10 year period.

While Muslim communities are better educated than a decade ago, there is a higher rate of unemployment and economic inactivity in comparison to the overall population, in part due to the fact that greater proportions of Muslim women looking after the home or the family.

A total of 18 per cent of the female Muslim population between the ages of 16 and 74 are looking after the home or family, which is three times as many as the whole population.

However, 29 per cent of Muslim women aged between 16 and 24 are in employment, compared with 50 per cent of the whole population.

Omar Khan, from the race equality think tank the Runnymede foundation, told the BBC Asian Network that the report made it clear Muslims do not have a problem with "British values" or identifying with Britain, and that is "nails some significant myths" about Muslims. He outlined the myths as "the number of Muslims [in the UK], which is often exaggerated; how proud Muslims are to be British; how well they fit in; and the narrative around British values". He said the report shows Muslims are proud to call themselves British and that they don't have allegiances to other countries in any other major way, or any confusion about where their identity lies.

But more important than numbers, facts and statistics is the way the discussion is framed. Even using the above numbers-based arguments to counter the position of Islamophobes falls into the bigotry trap. The logical implication of such an argument is that there is no need to fear Muslims only because there are more of 'us' than there are of 'them.' In reality, Muslims, irrespective of their numbers, are no more to be feared or hated than anyone else. Blood-curdling Faragian fantasies of thousands of newly-radicalised Jihadists pouring out of UK schools and mosques, intent on world domination, no-go Muslim ghettos, marauding bands of child-grooming paedophiles and sadistic pervert-fathers cheerfully hacking away at their daughters' genitals are, it's fair to say, somewhat non-representative of the UK's Muslim population.

It's also a little unhelpful when attempting to make political capital from so-called 'Muslim grooming gangs' to have one of your own party's Branch officers convicted of "... grooming children and possessing nearly 200,000 indecent images of children" as the *Bury Times'* Andrew Bardsley reported on November 25th, 2014. Yes, it seems Bury UKIPer Peter Entwistle rather let the side down when he "... spoke to children on MSN Messenger and other social network sites in a sexualised manner, asking them to commit sexual acts for his own satisfaction." Oops.

Bardsley's report explained that the fifty-two year old Entwistle called himself "the Naughty Doctor" and used a sexually explicit image of two women as his profile picture. 'Doctor' Entwistle engaged in, to say the least, inappropriate online exchanges with a thirteen year old girl and boy of twelve whom he thought was a girl.

When the long arm of the law finally caught up with the UKIP official his residence was found to contain numerous computers, USB drives and storage devices on which thousands of "indecent images" had been saved, along with a number of printed photographs and images.

When hauled before the beak Entwistle pleaded guilty to twenty-one offences including "possessing and distributing indecent images of children as well as inciting and the attempted inciting of children to commit sexual acts." He copped for four years and eight months porridge as well as lifetime membership of the nonces' club and his name entered onto that illustrious register which exists for such people.

It was revealed during his trial that his latest crimes weren't Entwistle's first time around the block. It seems that the good Doctor also had a previous conviction for indecent exposure dating back to the 1980s.

His brief did his best, of course, as briefs do, and read to the court a letter testifying to Entwistle's "good character." The letter was penned by none other than Alistair Burt, Tory MP for Bury North from 1983 to 1997, demonstrating little more than that Burt, whatever else he may be, is a pretty poor judge of character.

Judge Elliot Knopf tried to soften the blow, stating, "You are now 52-years-old, and you have, until these matters, led an exemplary life, which is attributed to by various letters I have received from people ranging from family, colleagues, the rector of churches and an MP."

Other details heard at the trial included Entwistle's treatment by a psychiatrist for depression and his history as a founder of UKIP in Bury and his Chairmanship of the branch from March 2011 to January 2013. It was not stated that the two things were connected.

Oh dear, Nigel. Don't you just it hate it when this sort of thing happens?

Chapter 3:
Birds of a Feather

"UKIP are a black hole for the ignorant to fall into."
JOHN LYDON

As if poor old Nigel didn't have his hands sufficiently full dealing with the calamity-prone sex offenders, homophobes and eugenics-enthusiasts inside his party, those outside UKIP presented him with additional challenges.

The first of these was the British National Party (BNP). The BNP was formed in 1982 by the Nazi John Tyndal, the former National Front leader, and comprised the merging of several far-right groups and currents. Despite frequent avowals of the party's non-racist nature, it restricted membership to "indigenous British", i.e. white people until 2010 when a legal challenge forced it to revise its ban of blacks, Asians and other ethnicities. The party's 2006 election manifesto was quite clear on the matter: "BNP activists and writers should never refer to 'black Britons' or 'Asian Britons' etc, for the simple reason that such persons do not exist. These people are 'black residents' of the UK etc, and are no more British than an Englishman living in Hong Kong is Chinese." Sadly, for the party, the law took a different view. Such a clause was discriminatory and the BNP was ordered by the court to admit non-white and non-indigenous applicants. One can only stagger in confusion through the contortions required to be in a 'non-racist' party banning black people from membership and then, possibly, die laughing at the surreal prospect of hoards of black men and women clammering joyfully to be — at last! — admitted to a party that openly called for their "repatriation."

From 1999 to 2014 the BNP was led by Nick Griffin who spent a great deal of time convincing observers that the BNP was no longer a racist party and that it had modernised and changed. Griffin's credibility in this regard was damaged somewhat by his 1998 conviction for distributing material likely to incite racial hatred, which earned the bungling would-be *Fuhrer* a suspended prison sentence. Further damage to the party's credibility was incurred when it became known that among its members and officers a large number of criminal convictions had been accrued. These included convictions for offences involving theft, violence, rape and sundry other niceties.

Griffin is a man not noted for incisive strategic thinking, or indeed any sort of thinking that might reasonably be described as rational, but he was nevertheless quick to recognise the opportunity UKIP presented to Britain's assorted racists, Nazis and reactionary hate-mongers. Griffin is now confined to the political scrapheap following his ejection from his evaporating fascist party but following the 2013 council elections in England and Wales, he posted his analysis of the results on the BNP's website.

Headed, *The Crossroads: Nick Griffin Examines the Key Lessons of the 2013 Council Elections,* the then BNP chief declared, "if, for whatever reason, anyone who thinks of themselves as a nationalist isn't prepared to join us and lend a shoulder to our wheel, then there is one other useful thing they can do: that is to join UKIP, or to put in effort in the social networks to find and influence those who have. Over the next few months, UKIP will sign up thousands of new, mainly newly politicised, members. Most of them are not merely patriotic, they are also instinctively, though at present totally incoherently, nationalist and racially aware."

This was advice his supporters were quick to follow and UKIP suddenly found itself home to a significant number of BNP defectors and entryists. Although in reality this was a process that had been underway for some time, prior to the elections. A week before the May polls opened, the UKIP boss grudgingly conceded that "one or two" of his party's candidates might also be members, or had been members, of the BNP.

UKIP fielded over 1,700 candidates and party staffers complained indignantly that they couldn't possibly vet that number of candidates in time. As Farage said, "I'll be honest with you; we don't have the party apparatus in a very short space of time to fully vet 1,700 people. I've no doubt amongst those 1,700 one or two will have slipped through the net that we'd rather not have had." He went on to reassure the electorate that such embarrassments wouldn't be occurring again: "When it comes to the General Election and the European elections, we have put in place a very rigorous testing procedure."

Presenting the bad news as a sort of administrative *faux pas* was a laughable attempt to lead the voters away from the real significance of the party's infestation by Griffin's BNP. Namely, how revealing it was that an out-and-out fascist party found UKIP so appealing in the first place.

The issue first emerged when it became known that one of UKIP's Cornish candidates, Susan Bowen, had previously been a member of the BNP. Leaping quickly into damage-limitation mode, UKIP officials quickly turfed the indignant Bowen from the party. The thwarted UKIP candidate was quick to refute accusations of Nazism. "I joined [the BNP] for the same reasons I joined UKIP — because I felt they would do something for the country. I am no Nazi and I was duped into joining the BNP. I didn't like my country being given away to foreigners." Possibly not the most convincing refutation she might have made.

UKIP had already been a very appealing home to ex-Nazis, well before 2013; so much so that the party had been forced, in 2008, to change its constitution to encompass an article explicitly banning BNP members — the only British political party who have needed to do so. The move has proved to be something other than a resounding success.

There can be few voters who doubt Farage is in possession of an enormous quantity of *chutzpah* but few would predict that it could extend to such outrageous lengths as, on the one hand, banning BNP members from joining UKIP while, at the same time, openly gloating at stealing voters from Griffin's discredited fascists. Facing in opposite directions simultaneously is a particularly useful political skill and one that Nigel Farage has mastered to an impressively high standard.

Speaking at Chatham House on March 31st, 2014, he said he was "quite proud" that his party had managed to pinch Griffin's voters. He continued, "What we did, starting with the Oldham by-election in the north of England, is for the first time try and deal with the BNP question by going out and saying to BNP voters; 'if you're voting BNP because you're frustrated, upset, with the changes in your community but you're doing it holding your nose because you don't agree with their racist agenda, come and vote for us'. I would think we have probably taken a third of the BNP vote directly from them, I don't think anyone has done more, apart from Nick Griffin on Question Time, to damage the BNP than UKIP and I am quite proud of that."

Quite the public service; all those poor non-racist BNP voters forced to hold their noses and vote for an openly fascist party because of "... changes in [their] community." What changes, one might ponder, could so upset a voter that he or she felt driven to vote for the BNP and then UKIP? Changing bin day to Fridays, perhaps? A high proportion of foreign potholes on Blighty's green and pleasant roads? No matter; Farage and his saintly UKIPers offered the average frustrated fascist a non-racist alternative.

The BNP, though, is but one strand of odious politics that UKIP effortlessly attracts. These days Britain First plays the role of street soldiers to UKIP's pound-shop Enoch Powells and would-be champions of the masses.

Britain First slithered onto British streets in 2011. Formed by former BNP member and anti-abortion activist, Jim Dowson, the organisation has a paramilitary wing called the Britain First Defence Force and is a classic fascist street-oriented movement. Like the now much-dimished English Defence League, Britain First places anti-Muslim harassment and intimidation at the centre of its activity. Invading mosques and terrorising Muslims — which it describes as "direct action" — the organisation is the fastest-growing far right formation in the UK. It also views UKIP very favourably and its members campaign tirelessly on behalf of Farage's party.

During the referendum campaign for Scottish independence the UKIP leader was jeered by pro-independence activists and ended up finding himself barricaded in a pub on Edinburgh's Royal Mile as demonstrators called him a racist and demanded, amusingly, that he 'go home', a sentiment with which Farage might have been expected to sympathise. Britain First's leaders were decidedly unimpressed. They announced that they would be placing "... hundreds of ex-British Forces" as well as "several armoured ex-Army Land Rovers" in the service of protecting Farage. The organisation also pointed out that despite the two organisations' status as rivals on the far-right, it recognised that the two were all "patriots together" and that it was, therefore, happy to "... put our men and resources at UKIP's disposal".

In subsequent by-elections, Britain First has canvassed and campaigned enthusiastically for UKIP with members of both organisations happy to pose with each other for cheerful photographs together on the campaign trail. Belated damage-limitation manoeuvres were instigated by UKIP officials while Britain First personnel responded with a nod-and-a-wink.

During the Rochester and Strood by-election, UKIP canvassers posed for photographs with Britain First's Jayda Fransen ('beautiful British name' as the Pub Landlord might have again remarked). While standing in the by-election herself Fransen is also the Deputy Leader of Britain First and played a leading role in her organisation's invasions of mosques. Or, as others might see it, the intimidation and harassment of Muslims.

Fransen is one of a number of Britain First members who claim UKIP is sympathetic to her group and claimed that it was UKIP personnel who'd requested she pose for photographs with them. UKIP claimed otherwise. Their people had been conned, apparently, and the party decisively rejected any link between itself and Fransen's far-right goons. A UKIP staffer protested, "A handful of our 200 campaigners on Saturday were photographed by Britain First without understanding the nature of the group and regret that very much. As we have discovered, this is a typical technique of Britain First, a form of political photobomb, to pretend that they have support elsewhere. They do not."

Britain First responded by telling its supporters that the UKIP line was merely "bluster for the media's sake", while on the group's Facebook page the group wrote, "UKIP at the ballot box, Britain First on the streets — a winning combination. Britain First has nothing but the utmost respect for UKIP's, but we are our own movement. The media is desperately trying to cause friction between us, but they won't succeed. We understand UKIP has to play the 'political game' so they have to distance themselves from us. We advise our supporters to ignore UKIP's necessary political manoeuvres when they condemn Britain First — it's all bluster for the media's sake. We wish Mark Reckless [UKIP's candidate, the former Tory MP] all the best in Rochester — UKIP at the ballot box, Britain First on the streets — a winning combination!"

One might expect UKIP, with its loathing and distrust of Europe, and given the outright racism and xenophobia of so many of its members, to be particularly averse to cosying up to foreigners and their organisations but one would be wrong. In October 2014 *European Voice* reported that Farage's European parliamentary current, the Europe of Freedom and Direct Democracy (EFDD) group — which had been staring collapse in the face, due to insufficient members — had been saved by a Polish far-right party joining. The *Voice* reported,

The Europe of Freedom and Direct Democracy (EFDD) group in the European Parliament has recruited a Polish MEP, just days after being forced to disband.

The group collapsed last week (16 October) after Iveta Grigule of Latvia defected. That meant that the EFDD did not have MEPs from enough member states to be officially recognised.

"The EFDD released a statement this afternoon (20 October) saying that it had recruited Robert Jarosław Iwazkiewicz, from the Polish far-right Congress of the New Right. He becomes the group's first Polish MEP, meaning it now has members from the requisite number of member states (seven). In June, the Congress of the New Right was in talks with Marine Le Pen of France's National Front about joining her planned far-right grouping."

There are three other MEPs from Iwazkiewicz's party in the European Parliament, but it is not yet clear if they will also be joining the EFDD. The party leader is MEP Janusz Korwin-Mikke, who caused outrage in July when he compared Europe's unemployed to African-Americans under Jim Crow laws in the American south.

"Four million humans lost jobs," he said during a debate about employment policy. "Well, it was four million niggers. But now we have 20 million Europeans who are the negroes of Europe. Yes, they are treated like negroes!" The vice-president who was chairing proceedings cut off his microphone. Korwin-Mikke has made controversial remarks in the past, including saying that women should not be allowed to vote.

Iwaszkiewicz has also been controversial in Poland. He appeared to endorse domestic abuse when he told the Wroclaw Gazette earlier this year that beating would "help bring many wives back down to earth".

The EFDD statement only refers to Iwazkiewicz joining the group, not his fellow party members. The statement quotes the Polish MEP as saying that he made the decision because he "wanted to help the vital and unique Eurosceptic group in the European Parliament. I joined the EFDD group because of two important values — opposition to EU bureaucracy and support for free markets so firmly supported by the UKIP delegation."

"To paraphrase Mark Twain, 'rumours of our death have been greatly exaggerated'," said EFDD co-leader Nigel Farage in the statement. There are conflicting versions as to why Grigule defected. The Parliament's political leaders say

she chose to leave the EFDD because her national party in Latvia is in talks to join a governing coalition, and did not want a party member in an extremist group. However, UKIP has insisted that Schulz [European Parliament President] told her he would strip her of her position as the head of a foreign delegation if she did not quit the group. No non-EFDD MEPs have publicly backed UKIP's version of events.

The group was formed by Farage in 2009 under the name Europe of Freedom and Democracy. Most of its MEPs came from UKIP, with a handful from six other countries. It stayed intact for the full 2009-14 term. Facing competition from Le Pen's efforts to create a new far-right group in the Parliament, UKIP joined forces with the anti-establishment Five Star Movement in Italy and changed the group's name, adding the word 'Direct'. In the new configuration, the 17 Italian MEPs shared the spotlight with UKIP's 24 MEPs, and it is now co-led by Farage and Five Star MEP David Borrelli.

Farage's fellow-traveller Korwin-Mikke certainly has the sort of form that would no doubt impress many UKIPers. Among his more interesting observations are that the difference between rape and consensual sex is "very subtle", and in a display of Holocaust-excusing claimed that Hitler was "probably not aware that Jews were being exterminated". The charming Pole is also on record demanding that the British minimum wage be "destroyed" and that women should not be allowed to vote. Strangely, the UKIP chief chose not to comment on his new buddy's unsavoury views but, instead, aimed his fire at Martin Schulz. The President of the European Parliament headed up a "banana republic" fumed Farage and was engaged in "manipulative backroom politics of the worst kind".

It's probably relatively easy for UKIPers to dismiss Korwin-Mikke as a rotten apple in an otherwise healthy barrel. Indeed Farage himself glibly excuses such people as the natural result of politics making for "strange bedfellows." Sadly, the Polish extremist is very far from being a rogue nutter in Farage's EFDD.

Magdi Cristiano Allam, an MEP from the exuberantly-named I Love Italy party, said that Islam wasn't a religion but an ideology and one "that preaches hatred, violence and death, but that is something we're not allowed to say". His comments were recorded on video and were made in response to a speaker at an EFDD "study day" who claimed Europe was "caving in" to Muslims and that Western civilisation is under threat of "Islamisation."

Another EFDD member is the Bulgarian Slavi Binev who was an invited guest and speaker at UKIP's annual conference in 2013. During an interview on his website, Binev states: "If Osama bin Laden symbolises the cruellest aspect of the Islam for the Americans, then the Muslim woman with her numerous children are his European equivalent."

Also a member of the EFDD is Frank Vanhecke, a Belgian MEP, previously a member of the Vlaams Blok which was forced to disband after a Belgian court found it to be in contravention of anti-racism legislation in 2002. Vlaams Blok experienced its greatest success when it switched the party's focus from its traditional far-right Flemish nationalism to an overt anti-Islamic and anti-immigrant agenda. The new philosophy was enshrined in the party's *70 Point Plan* which laid out measures for halting *all* immigration, the forcible — at gunpoint if necessary — repatriation of existing immigrants and to legally enshrine discrimination against immigrants in such areas as employment, housing and education. Vlaams Blok spokesmen drew a direct link between immigrants, especially Turkish and Moroccan immigrants, and crime and promised a zero-tolerance policy in respect of these demographics. Its furious anti-Muslim rhetoric was best seen in its 1993 election manifesto which stated that it saw Islam as a "doctrine which preaches holy war, assassination, forced conversions, oppression of women, slavery and extermination of infidels [which] will automatically lead to what we now call fundamentalism."

There was also a degree of political opportunism in the party's Islamophobia which was married to a very tough line on anti-Semitism. The Party openly courted Jewish voters who it felt would make natural allies in the fight against Muslims.

Vanhecke, who these days operates as an independent, also appeared on a platform with Nick Griffin during a student rally in 2010.

Next up is Morten Messerschmidt, of the Danish Peoples' Party who was convicted in 2002 for publishing material that linked rape, violence and forced marriage to multi-ethnic society.

Farage's one-time co-President of the EFD is the Italian Lega Nord MEP Francesco Speroni who, in 2011, was happy to act as apologist and defender of Norwegian racist mass-murderer, Anders Breivik. Speroni said that if Breivik's ideas "... are that we are going towards Eurabia and those sorts of things, that Western Christian civilisation needs to be defended, yes, I'm in agreement."

Speroni's party colleague, Gianliuca Buonanno, added to his organisation's unusual take on race relations by wearing blackface in the Italian parliament to protest at what he felt was the disproportionately generous amount of benefits available to those from ethnic minorities. *Molto elegante*, fellas.

Rowena Mason, one of the *Guardian*'s political correspondents, observed in the March 10th 2014 edition of the paper, that, "The rhetoric of some EFDD parties contrasts with Farage's emphasis that Muslims are welcome in UKIP. The UKIP leader has said he will not go into an alliance with Geert Wilders, the anti-Islam Dutch politician, or the French Front National and publicly rejected the suggestion of Gerard Batten, a senior Ukip MEP, that Muslims should sign a code of conduct."

Mason also quoted New York-based author Arun Kundnani (as well as lecturing at New York University, Kundnani is also the author of *The Muslims Are Coming: Islamophobia, Extremism and the War on Terror*): "The argument that Islam is not a religion but a totalitarian ideology is the standard line of the US far-right

Islamophobic conspiracy theorists. The term 'Islamisation' also has the same pedigree."

While one needn't be particularly surprised at a Muslim academic attacking UKIP's reasoning even some of Farage's former comrades have difficulty in justifying Nigel's alliances and partnerships. Mason, in the same article, also quoted one-time UKIP MEP Mike Nattrass who felt that he could not continue as a member of a Farage-led EFDD while it contained such overt racists and neo-fascists: "All that to me is outrageous. Yes, [Farage] did need the numbers to make up the group, But [they] don't need these people. The problem in that group is they don't all really share the same views. Ukip isn't anti-Islam actually, though it might be in league with people who are."

Mason's article contained some fascinating insights into the mindsets of Farage's European buddies. Vanhecke, for example, admitted sharing a platform with Nick Griffin but refuted suggestions he was an Islamophobe. Presumably without irony he claimed to be the type of man who has great respect for other cultures. Far from being a racist Vanhecke prefers to think of himself as a patriot albeit an admittedly right-wing one.

Strangely, though, he sees no conflict between his claims of eschewing Islamophobia and his insistence that Islam and Muslims represent a serious problem to Europe. Islam, to him, threatens democracy and equality between men and women. Because, as we all know, it's usually on the hard right that the most committed opponents of women's oppression are to be found...

Mason summed up: "UKIP's European alliances make for interesting study when set against the wider context of European far right growth. In the 2014 Euro elections a worrying number of voters ticked boxes for far right and openly fascist parties. 25% for Le Pen's Front National, 10% for Greece's Golden Dawn, 27% for the Danish People's Party, Holland's Party for Freedom in the Netherlands bagged 12% and the truly sinister Jobbik in Hungary polled

15%. The latter stating that Jews constituted a direct threat to the security of Hungary and should, therefore, be forced to sign a specially-created register."

Of course, such developments require little explanation. Economic meltdown and a general contempt for self-serving and unprincipled politicians are part of the problem and the easy scapegoats of immigrants and Muslims offered by the far right will account for most of their new-found popularity. To that we can add the post-Soviet era socialist parties willingly lining up behind their neo-liberal rivals' austerity measures.

While explanations are relatively easy to come by it's still difficult to ignore the chill engendered when considering that a quarter of France's people voted for — in the words of historian Dr. Tim Stanley — "... a party that is essentially a descendant of Vichy collaborationist fascism."

Writing in the *Telegraph* on May 28th, 2014, the good doctor went on to observe that "... a failure to confront history might lead to repetition. The countries that voted for the far-Right are generally those that have never fully admitted guilt or sought redemption for what happened in the 1930s and 1940s."

Pouring scorn on what he felt was French denial, Stanley sneered at the numbers of French citizens refusing to come to terms with their country's collaboration with the Nazis. Instead, "French history is clouded by the myth of the Resistance, of which practically every Frenchman claims to have been a member."

His thesis is that "the return of fascism in Europe is no surprise because it never went away. It probably never will."

In support of his contention, Stanley goes on to point to the Austrian Freedom Party which emerged from national liberation currents and ultimately merged with Nazism.

Holland, too, claims Stanley, while electing liberal governments at the same time was castrating people for the 'crime' of homosexuality. Apparently, eugenic studies and experiments were common across the Benelux countries. More widely known is Stanley's point that so-called liberal and centre parties openly and eagerly colluded with fascist parties, all over Europe, as the communist alternative was seen as a far bigger evil. Stanley concluded his *Telegraph* article by asking how does UKIP fit with the fascist history of Europe?

> *Awkwardly. Ukip attracts racists but is not a racist party. Its antecedents are the Right of the Tory Party — culturally reactionary, yes, but essentially libertarian and lacking a "blood and soil" definition of nationhood. They are much closer in spirit to the US Right, which defines itself by loyalty to a Constitution rather than a skin tone. Britain does have a fascist past, but it was never a mass movement and today only exists on the margins of society. It's more like organised crime than a serious politics. Not that Britain is unsullied; we still have the legacy of imperialism properly to confront.*
>
> *The bottom line is that here in the west we like to imagine that our society is superior to all others; that 'western values' automatically translate into democracy and human rights. But the reality is that Enlightenment exists alongside fascism, that our history is one where good and evil are finely balanced — with an occasional, and devastating, advantage to evil.*

Unlike those brown-skinned societies, one presumes, where good and evil are not so finely balanced? Nevertheless, Stanley might well be broadly correct where UKIP is concerned — it isn't a fascist party and possibly only the more unhinged elements of the Socialist Workers Party would insist that it is — but he doesn't dwell on the direction of travel. UKIP does indeed derive from the more reactionary and extreme elements of British Toryism but that tradition was itself once strongly attracted to Oswald Mosley's British Union of Fascists; as, of course, were many of Britain's aristocracy and ruling class.

Journalist Dave Osler offers an interesting analysis and sees things slightly differently: "I'm not sure 'essentially libertarian' is an accurate description of the right of the UK Conservative Party, in which the authoritarian/imperialist nostalgist strain was traditionally dominant and hasn't gone away. UKIP's claim to 'libertarianism' is joke; what sort of libertarians support immigration controls and oppose gay marriage? A better choice of adjective is 'Powellite'."

In November, 2014, in an article for *Left Food Forward*, Osler elaborated: "A sneering metropolitan elitist observation on the part of a self-confessed male moisturiser user this may be, but I can't help noticing that UKIP has achieved its breakthrough without offering the punters any clear ideological self-definition. That might just be one aspect of its success."

It's well worth quoting Osler in full offering, as he does, some interesting and pertinent analysis.

> Clearly it [UKIP] stands somewhere in the badlands to the right of the Tories, a fact that makes its advent as a serious political force all the more remarkable. Parties in that space have historically secured even fewer electoral victories than parties to the left of Labour, itself an extremely low bar.
>
> Yet somehow UKIP is on the cusp of becoming a fixture in Westminster life. Douglas Carswell and Mark Reckless are only the outriders of a likely double-digit sized contingent of UKIP MPs come next May.
>
> There is even a, mercifully slim, outside chance that it will be in government in little more than six months' time; the Daily Telegraph reports that David Cameron is open to a needs-must coalition with the very people he once sneeringly dismissed as 'loonies, fruitcakes and closet racists'. Effectively, we have entered terra nullis; a Conservative Party that has traditionally hegemonised the entire political space between the softer end of social democracy and a certain strand of hang 'em and flog 'em imperialist nostalgia politics must all of a sudden share the bandwidth.
>
> So let us try to define this upstart new arrival that little bit more closely. For ages UKIP just seemed odd, a fringe organisation designed to provide a protest vote option in that quinquennial euro bust-up nobody takes particularly seriously. Think Monster Raving Loony Party with a veneer of ostensible seriousness. Once it garnered support numbering into the

hundreds of thousands, commentators moved on to dismissing them as the respectable face of gin and Jag-belt racism. They were 'the BNP in blazers', as the cliché went. Wrong again. No Farage Youth are to be seen leafleting outside Jewish shops. UKIP is not a fascist or proto-fascist organisation, however hard some anti-racist campaigners try to hint otherwise.

But the confusion is understandable, given that even its own leadership has not seen fit to offer a succinct statement of UKIP's political philosophy. Nigel Farage himself tends to rely on an incoherent grab bag of ideas, picking up whatever golf club is suitable for the required stroke.

Sometimes he is Nigel the libertarian, claiming the imprimatur of John Stuart Mill on the back of the one quotation from On Liberty that everybody knows by heart. But it is an odd libertarian that has difficulty with the notion of equal marriage or the abolition of borders.

Sometimes he describes himself as 'green at heart' and then goes on to reveal that he does not accept the reality of anthropogenic global warming, which does rather bring his grasp of the science into question.

More useful, I think, is Farage's own admission that he is a Thatcherite but not a Conservative. His autobiography quotes Larkin's famous if patently dubious contention that sexual intercourse began in 1963; what is clear is that for Farage, politics began in 1979.

Yet even to describe UKIP as neo-Thatcherite doesn't hit the nail on the head. While the debt is obvious, Thatcherism was of its time and place, and that time and place is very different from where we are now. With unions already emasculated, nationalised industry already privatised and council housing already flogged off at a steep discount, a second showing of the movie is impossible. UKIP is accordingly reduced to being against things, most notably immigration and the EU, rather than for them.

Thatcher's politics were famously categorised by Marxism Today — a surprisingly popular political magazine during her period in office — as 'authoritarian populism'. It's almost tempting to resurrect the tag, with the inevitable coda of 'the second time as farce'.

What we have is populism in its most comedic form, a straightforward appeal to the wisdom of the imagined ordinary Brit, of no specified social class, combined with constant reiteration of the betrayals of 'the elite', syllogistically arranged to force the practical conclusion that it is time to throw the bums out.

UKIP under Farage may not be its finalised expression. Carswell has greater intellectual heft, a rudimentary agenda around direct democracy, and is said to be not unambitious. But the moment this party articulates a specific ideological vision, it will be harder to pull off the double act of promoting itself as the alternative to the Tories in Clacton and the alternative to Labour in Heywood and Middleton.

Let's not counter UKIP's appeal by floating calls for reduced access to benefits for EU migrants, as Rachel Reeves did in the Daily Mail earlier this week; the route-one football here is to repeatedly pin it down on NHS privatisation and scrapping maternity leave instead. The more concretely we paint them as a faintly pointless third-rate Thatcher tribute band hankering after the politics of 30 years ago, the more effective it will prove.

Under Farage UKIP has displayed a penchant for opportunism that stands out even amongst politicians where such elasticity is common. Simultaneously carrying the Thatcherite torch in the leafy Tory shires of the south east while, in the north west, proclaiming itself the only realistic defender of the working classes' culture, jobs and living standards, its lack of a fixed ideological base is, thus far, doing the party no harm. Much to the fury of the three main parties.

As Osler says, however, whatever it is — and whatever you say it is Nigel will insist it isn't — UKIP definitely occupies those badlands to the right of the Conservatives. However transparent, insincere and meaningless its courting of the industrial and former-industrial working class might be, it's working to at least a small degree. More remarkable is the rapidity with which Miliband, particularly, is falling into the trap and attempting to fight Farage on his own turf instead of marking out clear red water between him and Labour.

Chapter 4:
I'm Not Racist But...

"Most Nigerians are bad people"
UKIP poster-boy **Andre Lampitt**

If any one thing has garnered UKIP more column inches than anything else then that one thing is unquestionably the party's stance on immigrants and immigration. It has certainly replaced Europe as the party's defining characteristic in the eyes of the electorate. It offers yet more examples of the party's alleged official position being, shall we say, somewhat flexibly interpreted by its members. As UKIP have not yet produced an election manifesto — did I mention that, by the way? — we only have the party's website to help us. Where we read:

> We believe Britain must get back control over its borders, so that it can welcome people with a positive contribution to make while limiting the overall numbers of migrants and keeping out those without the skills or aptitudes to be of benefit to the nation.
>
> Regain control of our borders and of immigration — only possible by leaving the EU.
>
> Immigrants must financially support themselves and their dependants for 5 years. This means private health insurance (except emergency medical care), private education and private housing — they should pay into the pot before they take out of it.
>
> A points-based visa system and time-limited work permits.
>
> Proof of private health insurance must be a precondition for immigrants and tourists to enter the UK.
>
> UKIP recognises the benefits of limited, controlled immigration.
>
> UKIP will leave the EU, and take back control of our borders. Work permits will be permitted to fill skills gaps in the UK jobs market.

> *We will extend to EU citizens the existing points-based system for time-limited work permits. Those coming to work in the UK must have a job to go to, must speak English, must have accommodation agreed prior to their arrival, and must have NHS-approved health insurance.*
>
> *Migrants will only be eligible for benefits (in work or out of work) when they have been paying tax and NI for five years and will only be eligible for permanent residence after ten years.*
>
> *UKIP will reinstate the primary purpose rule for bringing foreign spouses and children to the UK.*
>
> *UKIP will not offer an amnesty for illegal immigrants or those gaining British passports through fraud.*
>
> *UKIP will return to the principles of the UN Convention of Refugees which serves to protect the most vulnerable.*

It's unfair, say UKIP loyalists, to brand the party as racist. They insist that racism plays no part in their immigration policy and that their stance is motivated purely, solely and only by what's best for Britain's economy. The arguments are familiar; we can't afford immigrants. Immigrants either take badly-needed jobs from indigenous Brits or spend all their time lounging around in ten bedroom-council houses, sipping champers from the skulls of British urchins, while relaxing in their hot-tubs watching cinema-scale plasma TVs, all funded by the lottery-sized mountains of benefits available only to immigrants; thanks to the Marxists in charge of the Department of Work and Pensions. Something that, I don't think I'm outrageous in suggesting, might come as a surprise to Iain Duncan Smith.

It's somewhat unfortunate that UKIP's apocalyptic vision of an immigrant-created economic dystopia is not just a bit, not just a little, but entirely at odds with reality. For example, immigrants are less likely than 'indigenous British people' to be claiming benefits and less likely to be living in social housing. According to the Centre for Research and Analysis of Migration: "European immigrants to the UK have paid more in taxes than they received in benefits, helping to relieve the fiscal burden on UK-born workers and contributing to the financing of public services."

A wide-ranging and in-depth research project, headed up by Professor Christian Dustmann and Dr Tommaso Frattini, the findings were published by the Royal Economic Society on November 5th, 2014 in the *Economic Journal* which showed that "European immigrants who arrived in the UK since 2000 have contributed more than £20bn to UK public finances between 2001 and 2011."

Additionally, as a labour resource immigrants had saved the UK nearly £7bn in education spending. The report claimed that from 2011 to 2013 "European immigrants from the EU-15 countries contributed 64% more in taxes than they received in benefits. Immigrants from the Central and East European 'accession' countries (the 'A10') contributed 12% more than they received."

Other findings that are likely to enrage the average UKIPer were that, since 2000, immigrants were 43% less likely than "indigenous" Brits to be claiming benefits or receiving working tax credits and were 7% less likely to be stealing council houses from more deserving Brits. It's a strange contradiction, which UKIP shows little desire to explain, that we are to believe that immigrants simultaneously come to the UK to live a life of idle luxury while at the same time stealing British jobs. The study blew such claims to smithereens.

Immigrants were, on the whole, better educated than their hosts and boasted significantly higher employment rates. The report gave a figure of 81%.

As well as saving the UK taxpayers nearly £7bn in education the report also found that "by contributing to 'pure' public goods (such as defence or basic research), immigrants arriving since 2000 have saved the UK taxpayer an additional £8.5bn over the same period."

Professor Christian Dustmann said:

A key concern in the public debate on migration is whether immigrants contribute their fair share to the tax and welfare systems. Our new analysis draws a positive picture of the overall fiscal contribution made by recent immigrant cohorts, particularly of immigrants arriving from the EU.

Responding to comments on our earlier report on this topic published last year, we performed extensive sensitivity analysis, which does not alter our main conclusions: immigration to the UK since 2000 has been of substantial net fiscal benefit, with immigrants contributing more than they have received in benefits and transfers. This is true for immigrants from Central and Eastern Europe as well as the rest of the EU.

When we additionally consider that immigrants bring their own educational qualifications whose costs are borne by other countries and that they contribute to financing fixed public services such as defence, these contributions are even larger.

To sum up, then, immigrants have made the UK economy wealthier to the tune of £20 billion. *Without* immigrants we'd be £20 billion worse off.

Some voters, then, might feel that UKIP's immigration policy is motivated by racism and bigotry, is economically incoherent, unrelated to reality and, if implemented, would be an unmitigated disaster for a country already holed beneath the waterline, thanks to toffs, bankers and the government's Eton Mafia.

All this is bad enough; it really doesn't need any further help from UKIP members offering their own interesting interpretations of what their policy means and how it should be implemented. Nevertheless, Nigel's followers insist on elaborating. For example, Councillor Victoria Ayling, once a member of the National Front, then a Tory and now UKIP's prospective parliamentary candidate (PCC) for Great Grimsby said, in 2013 "We must basically repatriate those that shouldn't be here. That's not quite policy yet. Maybe I should soften it a bit ... OK, send them back... I just want to send the lot back, but I can't say that." Not quite "policy yet" eh, Vicky? One wonders if Councillor Ayling knows something UKIP hasn't shared with the rest of us. Yet.

In addition to her take on her party's immigration policy, Ayling also displayed an unconventional understanding of environmental science, and created what I understand the younger generation term a 'facepalm' moment, when she asked a public meeting in Cleethorpes, on February 16th, 20015, "What happens when renewable energy runs out?"

But back to immigration. There was Mark Reckless, another Tory defector, who won the Rochester and Strood seat from, well, himself, I guess you'd say, given he was already the sitting Tory MP before resigning the seat and then winning it for UKIP, in the November 2014 by-election. Getting into a row with his former Tory colleagues regarding who were the bigger racists was an astonishing climax to his campaign. As the *Guardian* reported on November 19th, 2014: "The last day of campaigning in the Rochester and Strood by-election has exploded into a huge row about immigration, as Ukip's candidate was accused of using the language of forced repatriation and the Conservatives of campaigning like the British National party."

Reckless kicked off a bit of a row when he either let the cat out of the UKIP bag or went off-message. The former Tory reckoned that a plumber from Poland would only be allowed to remain in Britain for a finite period, should the UK end up leaving the EU. The party hierarchy slammed the UKIP Panzer into reverse, hastily assuring the voters that rounding up Polish tradesmen and shipping 'em all back was not quite how the party's immigration policy should be interpreted.

This appeared to upset the appropriately-named Reckless who responded by saying he'd been misunderstood and that his words had been twisted. No doubt by those cultural Marxists with which, in UKIP world, the establishment, media and related organs are stuffed. Of course Polish plumbers could stay. As long as they had the requisite work permit.

Amusingly, for neutrals and the left alike, he then stuck the boot hard into his former Tory chums, claiming they were "BNP-lite" as a Conservative election leaflet implied that people felt vulnerable and unsafe on their own streets, thanks to those pesky immigrants. He went on to point out that an associate of the Conservative candidate Kelly Tolhurst, a local Tory councillor, had claimed on his website that, "It is white, working-class Britons who have suffered the most. Now it is only the British National Party who represents them."

The good times rolled on. The Conservatives reacted with fury, accusing Reckless "and his minions" of lying about the council candidate, Ron Sands. Apparently, a full five years earlier Sands had taken to Facebook to publicly disassociate himself from Griffin's fascists.

Tollhurst rolled up her sleeves and got stuck in too. Telling Radio Kent that "It does disappoint me somewhat that Mark Reckless has chosen to lie on radio this morning about what I have said. What more can I say really? He's the one that's been very iffy and about his role and what he would like to do about immigration."

Reckless had been questioned about UKIP's stance regarding immigrants should Britain leave the EU. He responded, "I think in the near term we'd have to have a transitional period, and I think we should probably allow people who are currently here to have a work permit at least for a fixed period." When queried if that would mean deportation for Polish plumbers Reckless said: "People who have been here a long time and integrated in that way I think we'd want to look sympathetically at."

Protestations that UKIP's, and his, take on the subject was to control the amount of new immigrants and to avoid a system that favoured European immigrants over non-EU immigrants only served to stir up further controversy. Labour's Naushabah Khan also fancied a piece of the action: "Where would you stop, Mark?" she asked. "My family are migrants. Are we going to say they need to go back as well?"

It had all gone too far for Reckless as the Tories and Labour alike piled gleefully into the ruckus. Former Tory

Home Office Minister Damian Greene said Reckless had come "perilously close to repatriation" while Yvette Cooper piously opined, "To hear the language of repatriation coming from someone they [UKIP] hope will be their second MP is shameful. It's a policy that comes straight out of the last BNP manifesto and does not reflect British values." Missing an enticing open goal no one from the mass of feuding Tories and UKIPers bit back by reminding Cooper that such politics might reasonably have been suggested to have been approved by Labour, what with Gordon Brown's "British jobs for British workers" slogan.

A UKIP mouthpiece wearily defended the besieged Reckless: "Ukip's position on migration is entirely clear. We need to sort out our borders, and we cannot do so whilst we remain in the European Union. Those who are in this country lawfully, such as those from EU nations would have the right to remain. Those who are here illegally would have to apply for work permits."

Unsurprisingly, with the Tories and UKIP accusing each other of being the greater racists, immigration dominated the entire campaign. To add further controversy to what was, by any standards, an incendiary campaign, Tolhurst then had a pop at David Cameron berating him for the "hurt" immigration had brought to her beloved Kent. The Prime Minister was, according to Tolhurst, OK talking the talk but rather less than impressive walking the immigration walk. She thundered. "I wanted to bring the prime minister to this constituency to show him that uncontrolled immigration has hurt this area. I told him we need action, not just talk."

Tolhurst appeared to occupy a world, similar to that inhabited by UKIPers, where feckless immigrants arrive in the UK to live lives of unimagined luxury and wealth, at the expense of the natives, by greedily hogging all the goodies and services to themselves. One of her election leaflets stated that "Most people I know here have worked hard all their lives, played by the rules and paid their fair share, but we sometimes struggle to access the services we need because of uncontrolled immigration. Others don't feel safe walking down the high street of our town."

Mind you, even Reckless was eclipsed when Kent UKIP county councillor Trevor Shonk blamed immigrants for... the British being racist. The *Guardian*, from December 26th, kept an admirably straight face when it reported: "The UKIP leadership has moved to distance the party from remarks by one of its councillors claiming an 'overload' of immigrants had turned Britain into a racist country. Kent County Council UKIPer, Trevor Shonk, savaged both the Tories and Labour for letting in more immigrants than the UK could handle. On the BBC's World at One, he claimed, 'When I've done leaflets every shopkeeper, whether they are Asian or English-born, they're concerned about the influx. It hasn't been staggered; it's just overload. We haven't got the care homes, we haven't got the houses for our own.'"

UKIP's deputy chair, Suzanne Evans, did her best to nullify Shonk's crass bigotry. Shonk, we were told, simply "didn't express it as well as he could." She went on: "I think Britain is actually a very accommodating country and I don't think by any stretch of the imagination can be termed racist. I know what councillor Shonk meant. Perhaps he didn't express it as well as he could. There has of course been a massive increase in immigration, which people find incredibly difficult to deal with."

This was the latest in a flurry of controversial incidents involving prominent UKIPers. Just prior to Shonk's blunder was parliamentary hopeful Kerry Smith stood down as a UKIP candidate after he'd been outed for a string of racist and homophobic outbursts.

At the same time National Front veteran Martyn Heale was kept busy fending off journalists interested in his previous membership of the Nazi organisation in the 70s. With a somewhat disconcerting absence of irony UKIP's Suzanne Evans complained about media bias where UKIP was concerned. The almost wall-to-wall media coverage of UKIP has been a significant factor in the party's success in the polls but, somehow, Evans felt aggrieved when that coverage occasionally featured some tough questions: "The media reporting of Ukip is not fair. I think the establishment is very upset with Ukip and the fact that it is shaking the cosy status quo, the stitch-up the three old parties have had between them. Ukip is standing up for things that good, honest, decent people care about." This, of course, depends entirely on one's definition of "good, honest [and] decent".

UKIP election posters and broadcasts also seem to be something of a problem, where immigration is concerned. In one, a 'British worker' bemoaning the negative impact UKIP claims immigration has had on the UK turned out, somewhat unfortunately for the party, to be not so much British — actually not British at all — but in fact, an immigrant.

The case of Andre Lampitt proved to be instructional regarding the public face of UKIP's immigration policy compared to what its members privately feel. Oliver Wright informed *The Independent's* readers on April 24th, 2014, that: "Ukip has been forced to suspend the 'poster boy' of its European election broadcast, after it was revealed he had posted a series of vile racist comments on Twitter." UKIP's glossy promo flick which was shown on the BBC and ITV starred Mr. Lampitt. Strolling around a building site poor old Lampitt bemoaned the straights in which he'd found himself, thanks to alleged unlimited immigration from Europe. Commenting dolefully, Lampitt said, "Since the lads from Eastern Europe are prepared to work for a lot less than anybody else, I've found it a real struggle. It's getting hard to provide for my family."

It was, then, a bit unfortunate that Lampitt was revealed to be an immigrant himself. Hailing from Zimbabwe or as he prefers to call it — rather revealingly — Rhodesia. So far so embarrassing. But there was more. After a series of Tweets made by the Zimbabwean immigrant were brought to the attention of UKIP party bosses, yet another PR disaster befell Nigel's people's army. From March 2014, Lampitt Tweeted on a variety of topics, including Muslims, AIDS, Syria and enforced sterilisation. None of which could be said to be dripping with the milk of human kindness.

Regarding slavery: "Get over it, slavery was an act of war. You lost stop being so damn jealous and move forward." Muslims: "Muslims are animals their faith is disgusting their prophet is (a) pedophile". (sic) About Ed Miliband: "He is Polish and not British so how'd he know what's good for Britain?" Africa: "I was born and grew up in Africa please leave Africa for the Africans lets them kill themselves off don't go there." Syria: "When I voted they did not tell me they would spend our tax money on Syrians I'm sorry but this is unfair."

Embarrassed UKIP officials were forced to suspend Lampitt with a spokesperson stating: "We are deeply shocked that Mr Lampitt has expressed such repellent views. His membership has been suspended immediately pending a full disciplinary process." Awkward. Much.

The story is never-ending. On the day this book went to press the *Herald* in Scotland reported that "Jonathan Stanley, who has contested elections in his home city of Edinburgh and was until recently the party's head of policy in Scotland, said: 'This sectarian and racist filth [within UKIP] in Scotland needs cleaning up. It is a great threat to the Eurosceptic cause and civil society.'"

Farage himself has also acquainted himself with the quagmire that his party's immigration policy presents to the unthinking, the hard of thinking and the incapable of thinking. To most explosive effect during the now-legendary car-crash radio interview with LBC's James O'Brien in May, 2014. As Heather Saul reported for *The Independent:* "Nigel Farage's self-assured media persona rapidly came undone in a tense interview with LBC presenter James O'Brien on Friday, as the Ukip party leader was repeatedly challenged over his attitudes towards immigrants, allegations of racism and his expenses before his director of communications was forced to terminate the interview."

Farage had previously complained that when hearing foreign languages spoken on the tube it made him feel "uncomfortable."

"It was not until we got past Grove Park that I could hear English being audibly spoken in the carriage," the UKIP boss had said. O'Brien wondered if, then, when Farage's German wife spoke in her mother tongue, that he felt similarly discomfited. That was different, apparently, as Mrs. Farage could also speak English. To which O'Brien asked how Farage could possibly know whether the passengers on the train could speak English or not?

Of course, there was nothing racist about such a stance, insisted Farage: "What is racism? Is race about colour? Is race about race or is it about nationality? I made a comment there that wasn't intended to say any more than that I felt uncomfortable about the rate and pace of change." O'Brien responded: "You felt uncomfortable about people speaking foreign languages, despite the fact that presumably your own wife does when she phones home to Germany?"

"I don't suppose she speaks it on the train," Farage testily replied.

O'Brien then moved on to Farage's controversial assertion that he would feel uncomfortable if a Romanian family moved into the house next door to his, asking if the UKIP chief would feel the same way should the neighbours — like Farage's own offspring — turn out to be a "... group of German children" enquiring "What's the difference?"

Farage darkly, and with knowing emphasis, responded, "I think you know the difference. We want an immigration policy that is not just based on controlling not just quantity but quality".

When questioned about the seemingly endless numbers of UKIP members who had made outrageous and offensive statements, the clearly exasperated Farage complained,

"All anyone wants to talk about is the idiots in Ukip. Wherever we have found people who have had extreme, racist, unpleasant views we have unceremoniously got rid of them. To hold out the views of a handful of people as being representative of Ukip frankly is not the truth."

Saul's article continued:

> Yet O'Brien read out a Facebook post from a Ukip candidate suggesting that "poofters" might reconsider their sexual orientation if one was made an example of and shot, which had been posted three months before. In an awkward exchange, Farage was forced to admit he knew nothing about the tweet or the individual who tweeted it.
>
> The interview was brought to a close 22 minutes in by Patrick O'Flynn, the party's head of communications, after Farage was accused by O'Brien of "reverse-ferretting" over a promise to have his EU expenses and allowances audited, before enquiring if Farage would be willing to sign up to a transparency arrangement used by Labour MEPs, which he had to hand in the studio.
>
> When O'Flynn burst into the studio and interrupted, O'Brien explained: "This is Patrick O'Flynn, Ukip's Director of Communications and former political commentator on the Daily Express. Is this a friend in the media, or a member of the political class?" This came after Farage had been challenged earlier in the interview over a phrase where he discussed "members of the political class and their friends in the media". O'Brien pointed out Farage writes columns for both The Independent and The Express, and regularly appears on Question Time.

Those pesky Romanians would continue to constitute something of a quagmire for Nigel. A few days later the BBC reported: "Nigel Farage has defended controversial remarks he made about Romanians, saying people would be right to be concerned if a group moved in next door. The UKIP leader was speaking to the BBC the day after appearing to say he had been wrong, because he was tired."

We've all been there. Tough shift, hard day and, obviously, you'll slide into a bit of a racist outburst; just an unfortunate side-affect of fatigue.

The report continued: "On four occasions in an interview with the BBC's Political Editor Nick Robinson, Nigel Farage was offered the opportunity to apologise but refused. 'It was only when I asked him if it would be right to say that you should be worried if Nigerians or Jamaicans or Irish people were your neighbours that his position started to shift,' said Robinson."

Unsurprisingly, Farage was met with accusations of racism. Furious Labour MP David Lammy, himself of immigrant stock, said that he "... remembered a context in which some people said you don't want these people living next to you. What Nigel Farage said over the weekend was racist, so I'm clear, he's a racist."

Even the Prime Minister was forced to add his two bob's worth, commenting that Farage had "really pretty unpleasant things" while Ed Miliband, not be left out, offered that Farage had been guilty of making a "racial slur." Farage eventually conceded that "If I gave the impression in that interview that I was discriminating against Romanians then I apologise certainly for that. I do not wish for people to feel in a discriminatory manner towards Romanians but I do say there is a very real problem here that everybody else has run away from, brushed under the carpet, the whole organised crime element and the impact that has had on London and other parts of the country. That is a serious issue."

Apparently, the O'Brien interview had been a cause for regret with Farage saying he'd wished he hadn't said "you know what the difference is" when questioned about the difference between a Romanian family or German children moving in next door to him. "I am apologising for not taking the question full on and for giving the impression that by saying 'you know what I mean' there was somehow an agenda underneath."

Perhaps not the most sincere apology, given that during his interview with Nick Robinson he wondered "Can we just have an honest appraisal of what has happened to post-Communist Romania? Across the whole of the European Union, amongst all twenty-eight member states, 7% of all crime is committed by 240 Romanian gangs. The reality is people would be concerned. If we stop the gangs coming in through Dover and elsewhere there would be no need to be concerned."

Quickly clarifying his thoughts, he added: "I didn't say people should be concerned, I said they would be concerned. That is a reflection of reality. But I want to change that so people wouldn't be concerned, and we can do that by getting back proper border controls."

Later, when speaking on the BBC's Newsnight, further backtracking was required with Farage admitting he had been wrong to state in the *Daily Telegraph* that 7% of all crime in Europe was the responsibility of Romanians. Apparently, what he'd really meant to say was that 7% of "criminal networks" in Europe were Romanian: "It was criminal networks, not crime."

7% seems to be a rather odd figure. Or put another way, 93% of all European crime is, presumably, *not* committed by either Romanians or Romanian "criminal gangs" — whatever the difference between the two might be. The gospel according to Nigel is that "It's all a question of scale; on a pro rata basis the biggest problem is coming from Romania." Oh. Work that one out if you can.

In any event, Farage had neatly alienated any Romanians, a point underscored by Doctor Tommy Tomescu, a Romanian and candidate for the Europeans' Party. Dr. Tomescu said that London's Romanians were not too impressed with Nigel Farage. The BBC reported: "I think he [Farage] was desperate to be sure that he came in first place and pushed too much," he [Tomescu] said. This was not the first time that Mr Farage had offended Romanians, he added, suggesting that the UKIP leader had told "lies" about the number of his countrymen and women who were likely to come to the UK when immigration controls were lifted at the start of the year. "Some people just say it is the five-year electoral cycle but it is unbelievable what has happened," he said. He urged the UKIP leader "to change his way of thinking". "[Farage] said he made a mistake but he does not show a deep recognition that it was wrong. He needs to apologise but to apologise in a credible way."

There was further controversy when, on February 16th, Channel 4 broadcast a 'docu-drama' looking at what a UKIP government might mean for the UK. Furious party members and supporters complained to both Channel 4 and the broadcasting watchdog OfCom. Some, puzzlingly, even before the programme had aired. In a perfect example of just because Dan Hodges says something it doesn't necessarily mean it's wrong, the scourge of the left wrote in the *Telegraph* on February 17th, 2015: "Why do racists object so vehemently to being called racist? I genuinely don't get it. They've crossed the line, morally and intellectually. Decided to articulate their prejudice openly and honestly. And yet for some reason, when confronted with their racism, most suddenly shrink back, and adopt a pose of wounded innocence. 'Me? Racist? Just because I keep slagging off the blacks and the immigrants? How dare you!'"

What prompted Hodges' question was the screening by Channel 4 of the programme entitled UKIP: the First 100 Days, which was described by Farage as "A biased, partisan depiction of the only party that Believes in Britain." He was joined in his condemnation of the programme by Hodges' *Telegraph* colleague Ben Lawrence who fumed "The First 100 Days was laced with the same metropolitan snideness that destroyed MP Emily Thornberry's career when she tweeted a picture of a St George flag-covered house last year."

Hodges disagreed and delivered a forensic and reasonable explanation of why Channel 4 had actually done a pretty realistic job of portraying some of the things likely to occur in the event of UKIP ever forming a government. Hodges explained,

...the basic narrative is built around four basic conceits — Ukip win a majority, and then introduce three flagship policies: EU

71

withdrawal, a crackdown on immigration and a Festival of Britain bank holiday. Within 100 days these policies collide and chaos descends.

Now, I'm sure no one in Ukip will argue with the first premise, (though I don't quite see how Nigel Farage is supposed to have cobbled together a working majority on 36 per cent of the vote). So we can park that one.

The second is that Ukip's election, and withdrawal from the EU, creates economic turmoil. Which is of course true. If we did wake up to Prime Minister Farage on 8 May, the pound would indeed go into freefall and pandemonium would indeed descend on the stock market. That's not supposition, it's fact. The idea that major firms would withdraw from the UK is more open to debate, but probable. That major planned overseas investments in the UK would be deferred is inevitable.

The third conceit, a major immigration crackdown, is simply stated Ukip policy. Why Ukip spokesman are up in arms about images of Ukip border force officers kicking down doors is beyond me. It's what they and their supporters demand every day of the week. They also seem outraged at the fact that in the program this immigration crackdown is shown to create disorder on the streets. Well, it would. And I know it would, because if Ukip followed through with the policy of forced repatriation it floated during the Rochester by-election, I'd be one of the people out on the streets causing it.

The final proposition is that Ukip holds a day celebrating "Britishness". Now I personally think it's a daft idea, because as we've seen over he course of countless tedious debates on the subject, Britishness is utterly impossible to define. But Ukip advocate such a festival, as do politicians of many parties. And although in the film its used as a catalyst for Deepa Kaur's realisation that she is betraying her personal values in pursuit of her career, it's made clear the celebration is embraced by hundreds of thousands of good, honest, decent Brits.

Hodges concluded by wondering what on earth UKIP's problem with the docu-drama was. He suggests that Channel 4 had held up a mirror to UKIP supporters and they disliked intensely what they'd seen. The inevitable consequences of their politics could quite easily and credibly lead to the outcomes posited by the programme-makers but that "... as soon as anyone turns round and confronts them with that politics, they cry foul. Every week, Nigel Farage and his party launch a fresh attack on migrants. They launch a fresh attack on the EU. They wrap themselves in the flag — look at Farage's McCarthyite new slogan that implies a failure to support Ukip is in some way unpatriotic. And yet when Channel 4 produce a program showing Ukip withdrawing from the EU and cracking down on immigrants and wrapping themselves in the Union Jack, they go running off to Ofcom. Channel 4 have clearly struck a nerve."

And yet for all the controversy UKIP's immigration policy has seen rain down on the party, it is still holding up well in the polls with around a ten percent share of the vote and, much more importantly, it continues to heavily influence both the Tories and Labour. It seems that every time Nigel Farage announces some tougher measures to deal with immigration and immigrants, both David Cameron and Ed Miliband tumble over each other to announce they'd be even tougher. Making plans for Nigel, indeed.

For the Tories, this is home turf and steering the party even further to the right is as natural as the sun rising in the morning. There are modern precedents. Prior to the 1979 General Election, the Thatcher-led Tories were losing ground to the National Front and promptly responded by stealing the NF's rhetoric and successfully tempted wavering Tories and hard-line racists, often the same thing, of course, back into the Tory fold. So it is with Cameron and Farage. Labour, however, still claims to be different. It isn't, sadly, which prompted its David Lammy MP to condemn his party for trying to "Out-UKIP UKIP." Lamiat Sabin reported the Labour MP's disgust in *The Independent* on January 28th, 2015. An MP hoping to replace Boris Johnson as Mayor of London next year has criticised the Labour Party for trying to "out-kip UKIP" with an immigration leaflet using "inflammatory rhetoric".

Lammy was quick to take to Twitter posting a photo of the offending leaflet which boasted that Labour would take a "tough new approach to immigration." The tone and implication of the message, not least its language, had upset some of the Labour MP's constituents, apparently. Some of its themes were the sort of things one might expect from the Tories. It clearly enraged Lammy that Labour were stooping to such measures. Perhaps he'd been visiting Mars when Jack Straw had been Home Secretary?

Still, snidey references to nurses not speaking English and the stark declaration that "The Tories have lost control of our borders and have no idea who is coming in or out of the country" suggested Labour have few qualms following both the Tories and UKIP into the gutter. The leaflet continued: "That's why Labour will bring in 1,000 extra border staff to count people in and out of the country as well as fingerprint checks to clamp down on illegal immigration. People who rely on public services have a right to expect that staff, like nurses and care workers, can speak English. That is why Labour will make sure that all frontline public sector staff can speak English."

Lammy's problem, though, and it's one that most Labour Party members face, is that Labour *is* as bad as the Tories on these questions, while shamelessly pretending that it isn't. Labour candidates are often required to face in two different directions at the same time.

And thus it was for comrade Lammy. Sabin continued for *The Independent*:

> Despite disagreeing with the "tough rhetoric" of the leaflet, Mr Lammy said he is for policies such as a minimum of two years before a migrant can claim benefits if they have already paid into the system. Mr Lammy said: "Our policies on immigration are sensible and balanced. This leaflet, with its talk of being 'tough on immigration' and having 'lost control of our borders' is neither of those things. These flyers have been going through letter boxes in my constituency — one of the most diverse in the country — and the response has not been positive. I have had numerous calls and emails complaining about the offence

that they have caused. People are questioning this caricature of nurses who don't speak English. Many of my constituents are nurses and they are telling me that there is no way they would have passed their three-year course if they didn't speak good English. What we should not be doing is taking part in a race to the bottom with the Tories and with Ukip to see who can come up with the toughest rhetoric on immigration. I will be making the case for immigration strongly and proudly in the coming months," Mr Lammy added.

A Labour spokesman said: "We are proud of our diverse and outward-facing country, where people have come from abroad over many generations to build Britain's businesses, work in our public services and contribute to this country but immigration reforms are needed to ensure the system remains fair."

It's a tough gig allowing UKIP to drag your immigration policy to the right and onto Farage's turf while piously opining that you're doing no such thing and then complaining when others accuse you of doing just that. Labour politicians, however, are certainly giving it their best shot. Tony Blair successfully out-Toried the Tories so Miliband and co evidently think out-UKIPing UKIP is worth a punt.

Good luck with that, Ed.

Chapter 5:
Sluts

"Business owners should be free to turn people away for whatever reason they choose; be they gay, black or a woman."
UKIP councillor **Donna Edmunds**

In 2006 Farage was elected leader of UKIP. Top of his list of priorities was to continue widening UKIP's influence and representation at all governmental levels; local, national and European.

It was around this time that the party really made its first serious steps away from the single-issue Europe-focused foundations that had defined its existence and into the populist far-right vehicle that exists today. His maiden speech was the sort of tub-thumping attention-grabbing entertainment which had first established his profile in the European Parliament. UKIP was now, he told delegates, "at the centre-ground of British public opinion" — which wasn't far off the mark, given how far to the right the British body politic had been dragged over the preceding thirty-plus years — and the "real voice of opposition".

The impact was immediate and in 2009 the new-look UKIP came second only to the Tories in that year's Euro elections, with the second-ever highest share of the vote — over two million — Labour and the Liberal Democrats were pushed into third and fourth places respectively.

From then until now it's been fascinating watching the party extend its appeal to sections of the electorate other than the Eurosceptic and Europhobic. Farage's party see vote-catching in a very different light to, say, Labour which, for years now, has pretty much concentrated on not only ignoring its core vote but actively espousing policies that damage it; instead, preferring to chase the mythical approval of so-called 'Middle England.' The reasoning being that traditional Labour voters can be, at best, ignored with the party secure in the knowledge that blind loyalty will see Labour supporters turn out and vote for the ebola virus as long at it's decked out in a red rosette. Scotland, we now know, has delivered its verdict on such treatment.

Of course, UKIP is equally sneering in its treatment of the voters and in the case of women one can only stare in wonder at the disdain with which UKIP treats a demographic that comprises slightly over half of the total population of the UK.

UKIP's previous where women are concerned is quite something. Among its members' considered observations on female emancipation included a possible ban on women wearing trousers because, at least according to one of its biggest donors, Demetri Marchessini, their legs were "essentially sexy."

Possibly a dubious compliment by comparison to the wisdom of Yorkshire MEP Godfrey Bloom whose general view was that womankind comprised mainly "sluts" who were less than fastidious when cleaning behind the fridge. A suggestion that cost the gentleman his party's whip.

The *Telegraph's* Victoria Lambert was moved to liken UKIP to "the political equivalent of that pompous twerp at the school disco who is so scared of girls he can only patronise them while, in the hope of appearing sophisticated, treating them to a port and lemon."

Lambert pondered the mystery of the potential female UKIP voter: "it is difficult to fathom why any woman — even the handful pledged to stand in those bullish purple colours at the next election — would vote Ukip, because the clues to how the party feels about women keep coming, don't they?"

The columnist went on to examine the furore that had blown up around one-time rising star Natasha Bolter who had claimed the Party's General Secretary, Roger Bird, had sexually harassed her. Bolter responded by stating that the two had engaged in a consensual relationship. Lambert wrote: "We may never know whether Bird was using his position within the party to encourage Bolter to have an affair, but we now know he is the sort of man who doesn't like girls in jeans. According to Bolter, when the pair met for dinner, he insisted on buying her a £169 dress from Ted Baker and some — dear God — matching shoes, before telling her she 'now looked like a girl who could get in a taxi'. Presumably, back in 1955."

Then there was Farage's objection to breast-feeding mothers. Purely in the interests of consideration and sensitivity, you understand. The UKIP leader was only concerned that some unnamed persons, definitely not he, of course, might be offended by the "ostentatious" displays of breastfeeding in which mothers are known to engage. He declined to elaborate on what he meant by "ostentatious" leaving those with rather more vivid imaginations to picture feather-crowned huge-breasted amazons towed by Village People lookalikes on *Mardi Gras* floats to their nearest Starbucks, whereupon fireworks were ignited in welcome as wriggling infants gorged themselves on the mammalian nectar.

One was forced to wonder if breast-feeding mothers were as offensive to UKIPers as working ones, given that Farage felt maternity pay was a needless burden on small businesses and that only those "young, able women who are prepared to sacrifice the family life and stick with their careers" were deserving of the party's approval.

Lest loyal UKIPers feel such ruminations are the province of lefty, hirsute lesbians or feminists — probably the same thing in UKIP world. It's instructive that the party's stance on women even irked some of its own female members. As Marta Andreasen, who ended up defecting to the Tories, pointed out, Farage "doesn't try to involve intelligent professional women in positions of responsibility in the party. He thinks women should be in the kitchen or in the bedroom."

Victoria Lambert concluded her remarks in the *Telegraph* by considering that "… women who care about pay, pensions and family rights, women who want to contribute to debate on these issues, will vote for parties that take them seriously. Vote for Ukip? Show me the turkey who would vote for Christmas."

Unfortunately lots of turkeys do vote for Christmas. How else does Ms. Lambert think Tory governments get elected? Inexplicably, some turkeys not only vote for Christmas but actively clamour to assist in their own stuffing. Yes, I'm talking to you, Sanya-Jeet Thandi.

The female and Asian UKIPer was the head of the party's youth wing, itself a quite disconcerting concept; pubescent mini-Nigels demanding their schools take action at Romanian pupils stealing everyone else's dinner money? Georgia Graham told the *Telegraph's* readers on May 13th, 2014, of Thandi's "terrifying" experiences while attempting to organise UKIP's junior "racists." Georgia Graham said to *Telegraph's* readers "A British Asian leader of Ukip's youth wing has quit the party, branding it 'racist' and 'terrifying'.

It transpired that Sanya-Jeet Thandi, once tipped as a future UKIP leader (presumably to the chagrin of the sluts-behind-the-fridge tendency), felt that UKIP had strayed from its founding principles and was now cynically appealing tot the "stupidity of ignorant anti-immigrant voters for electoral gain". Something unlikely to have surprised anyone apart from Ms. Thandi herself.

The former party star resigned and then demanded other UKIP supporters join her in boycotting the forthcoming Euro and council elections. Thandi felt that her former party's one-track obsession summed up everything that was wrong with the latest incarnation of UKIP.

Farage had made some effort to cleanse the party of its racist image, not least in a tasteless photo-opportunity where he posed with forty supporters from various ethnic minority backgrounds. He pleaded: "I don't care what you call us, but from this moment on, please do not call us a racist party." None of which was "good enough" for Thandi who felt such initiatives were far too little, too late and stood little chance of cancelling UKIP's "racist populism."

In that she was surely correct as the fracas surrounding one UKIP loyalist's suggestion that Lenny Henry should emigrate to a "black country" rather underlined.

Graham summed up her *Telegraph* article on Thandi by writing:

> Miss Thandi, who grew up in Kent, became one of Mr Farage's biggest cheerleaders, telling The Times that Mr Farage was 'a babe' and describing Godfrey Bloom as 'cute and so kind and hilarious, he just says things for the reaction. Lovely guy but a bit misunderstood'.
>
> However, announcing her resignation on the Guardian website Miss Thandi said people with 'racist views had now been slipping through Ukip's checks time and time again.' She wrote: 'In order to convince society they are not racist they need to stop giving positions in the party to people with racist views. It is not good enough to say that these individuals just slipped through the net, time and time again. Yes, Ukip is still a relatively young party. No, that is not an excuse to allow racists to stand for election. Nor is it an excuse to exploit the ignorance in British society and indulge the racist vote by telling them 'they'll take your jobs'."

Better late than never, one supposes. Mind you, it would be dishonest to imply Thandi was the only UKIP turkey.

Farage, whatever his detractors say about him, is not a stupid man and he clearly recognised that the party needed to seriously address its appalling orientation where women are concerned. The problem, however, lies in keeping the more traditionally-inclined male members on board while attempting to make UKIP a more attractive vehicle for what UKIPers would no doubt describe as the fairer sex. Something Nigel, somewhat ham-fistedly, both conceded and defended as *The Independent's* Andy McSmith recorded on October 8th, 2014:

81

Nigel Farage has admitted that Ukip is "blokeish" and has a women problem — before going on to prove it by asking: "What do you want me to do? Go sell flowers?"

Speaking after he had posed for photographers on top of a Chieftain Mark 10 tank while campaigning in Middleton in Heywood, in Lancashire, the Ukip leader said: "I am not going to pretend to reach out to female voters or voters of all different denominations. We're one country, we're one people and this party is making huge progress. The problem with female voters and Ukip is that, over the last 5 to 10 years, at times, on a very bad day, we've looked a bit blokeish, a bit like a rugby club on a day out and I'm probably the most guilty person of all ... The pub and everything else. It's true, it was a very male dominated party in every aspect."

That admission does not mean that the Ukip is proposing to change his ways. "What do you want me to do? Go sell flowers?" he said. But he claimed that matters had improved this year. Godfrey Bloom, who created a sensation at Ukip's 2013 conference by jokily calling a room full of women 'sluts' because they did not clean behind their fridges, has been disowned by Farage and is no longer an MEP. Ukip also fielded more woman candidates in 2014.

But polling evidence suggests that Ukip's appeal to women voters is still limited. One poll in Middleton and Heywood, where Labour is defending the seat left vacant by the death of Jim Dobbin, showed Ukip ahead of Labour by 41 per cent to 38 per cent among male voters, but trailing with only 21 per cent support among women.

Unfortunately, Farage has been somewhat hindered by the contributions of his male colleagues and supporters. Demetri Marchessini unhelpfully suggested that women couldn't possibly be raped by their husbands. As well as offering some considered opinion on the subject of date rape: "There's no such thing."

Marchessini, a millionaire businessman and UKIP donor, explained, "When you get married you promise to look after the other person for the rest of their life. You certainly don't promise that you're going to put them in jail. If you make love on Friday and make love Sunday, you can't say Saturday is rape. Once a woman accepts, she accepts and especially when she makes a vow on her wedding day."

Clearly on something of a roll Marchessini was happy to elaborate and expand his authoritative commentary into the area of homosexuality and the mores of gay men. The *Guardian's* Nicholas Watt informed the paper's readers on April 30th, 2013 that Marchessini, "... said that gay men are incapable of experiencing love. He said: 'There's no love, only lust, and also the physical actions that they do are completely different. They go out at night and they pick up five, ten, fifteen different partners in one night. Is that love? They are not husband and wife. They are roommates and both of them go out cruising. There is no such thing as fidelity in homosexual relationships. They just all go out looking for action. That's the way it is.'"

Farage was forced to admit that, on balance, accepting donations from Marchessini was perhaps not the most astute political move.

UKIP's opponents clearly saw an obvious weakness that needed to be exploited and prior to the 2014 Euro Elections James Bloodworth administered a brutal smack-down for *Left Foot Forward*. He wrote:

> *Thinking of voting for UKIP tomorrow? If you care even a jot about the rights of women, think on. Here are 15 reasons why women (and men who believe in equality of the sexes) should sooner drink poison than vote for the Kippers tomorrow.*
>
> 1. *Nigel Farage on women: "Godfrey's [Bloom, former UKIP MEP] comment that 'no employer with a brain in the right place would employ a young, single, free woman has been proved so right. With this lunacy, that if you have children you get three months paid leave off work, or six months paid leave off work — he absolutely got it spot on."*
>
> 2. *UKIP want to scrap paid maternity leave (in line with Lesotho, Swaziland, the US and Papua New Guinea).*
>
> 3. *UKIP want to make it legal for employers to discriminate on the basis of gender (as well as race).*
>
> 4. *This would also entail the scrapping of employment regulations against sexual harassment and safeguards for*

part time and irregular workers, the majority of which are women.

5. Nigel Farage informed City high flyers that they are "worth less" to employers if they become mothers or that motherhood is a lifestyle choice.

6. Patrick O'Flynn, MEP Candidate, also say that pregnant women in the workplace are a "disaster".

7. UKIP's MEPs have consistently failed to represent the interests of women. They have voted against or simply not turned up to key votes in the European Parliament on ensuring equal pay, combating violence against women and ruling out FGM, to name but a few.

8. Since the 2009 European Election UKIP's only two female MEPs, Nikki Sinclaire and Marta Andreasen have both left the party. Andreason said Farage "doesn't try to involve intelligent professional women in positions of responsibility in the party. He thinks women should be in the kitchen or in the bedroom". Nikki Sinclaire won an Employment Tribunal claim for sex discrimination against the party.

9. Roger Helmer, UKIP MEP and candidate in the Newark by-election, said, "Rape is always wrong, but not always equally culpable."

10. Godfrey Bloom, a former UKIP MEP, was not reprimanded for hugely sexist statements such as, "[feminists are] shrill, bored, middle-class women of a certain physical genre" and, "Women, in spite of years of training in art and music — and significant leisure time in the 18th and 19th Centuries — have produced few great works".

11. Stuart Wheeler, the party's treasurer, said that women were "absolutely nowhere" when they compete with men in sports where they are not physically disadvantaged. He said, "I would just like to challenge the idea that it is necessary to have a lot of women or a particular number on a board... Business is very, very competitive and you should take the performance of women in another competitive area, which is sport where [men] have no strength advantage."

12. In November 2013, UKIP MEP, Stuart Agnew said (in a debate on women in the boardroom) that "Women don't have the ambition to get to the top, something gets in the

way. It's called a baby... Those females who really want to get to the top do so."

13. *David Chalice, a senior party official in Exeter, has voiced his belief that women should stay at home and that "cash-strapped Moslems" should have multiple wives.*

14. *Demetri Marchessini, the party's sixth-largest individual donor in 2013, claimed women should be banned from wearing trousers because they "discourage love-making".*

15. *Need I go on?*

Yes, things were getting out of hand and the matter needed addressing as a matter of utmost urgency and what better way of doing so than promoting more women to the party's top echelons? Perhaps predictably, but no less cringingly, Farage's female appointments were quickly dubbed 'Farage's Fillies.' Here's Graham again for the *Telegraph*, from July 25th, 2014: "After weeks of eerie quiet on the Ukip front Nigel Farage last night reshuffled his previously non-existent 'cabinet'. Mr Farage mimicked the Prime Minister's technique of live-tweeting the individual appointments — using the Twitter hashtag 'UKIPShuffle' — and, like David Cameron, used the pre-election shake-up to bring in many more women to his top team."

Things were getting serious. Black and ethnic minority UKIP voters were as rare as a politician's honour and support for the party among women was found to be "weak." The party desperately needed to widen its base of support and do something drastic to bring women voters on board. Graham noted: "Matthew Goodwin and Robert Ford, authors of the first authoritative study of the modern Ukip, said: 'Make no mistake, this [was] a revolt dominated by white faces, blue collars and grey hair: angry, old, white working-class men who left school at the earliest opportunity and lack the qualifications to get ahead in 21st-century Britain'."

Helpfully, Graham went on to provide thumb-nail biog sketches of UKIP's new female movers-and-shakers:

Diane James, South East MEP, Justice and Home Affairs: she ran in the Eastleigh by-election, and apologised in February last year when, as one of the candidates, she linked Romanian immigrants with a natural propensity towards crime. At the time she said: "On 1 January 2014 the floodgates will open for Bulgarian and Romanian citizens [to come to Britain]. We are not just talking about pressure on services from immigration but also, and I have to say it, the crime associated with Romanians."

Margot Parker, East Midlands MEP, Small Business: elected in 2014 she was educated at De Montfort University where she read Law. She opposes the smoking ban because it has contributed to "the demise of pubs" and she fears the Government plans to ban e-cigarettes in pubs and clubs. A local businesswoman who impressed Ukip's hierarchy with her spirited campaign in the Corby and East Northants by-election 18 months ago, She was elected as an MEP for the East Midlands at the recent European elections.

Jane Collins, Yorkshire MEP, Employment: she previously worked with Godfrey Bloom, the gaffe-prone former MEP and stood for Ukip in the Barnsley and Rotherham by-elections.

Mr Bloom quit Ukip after he joked that a group of UKIP women who did not clean behind their fridges were "sluts". She appears to hold similar views to her former boss, whom she succeeded as MEP in Yorkshire and North Lincolnshire. She told the Hull Daily Mail of Mr Bloom: "I am pleased he has not left the party, he is being incredibly supportive. As for the 'slut' remark, I was there and everyone in the room took it as a joke."

Louise Bours, North West MEP, Health: a newly elected MEP, the professional singer and actress went under the surname of her Dutch father "van de Bours" until 2013. Before becoming Mr Farage's resident health expert she appeared in TV series such as Band of Gold, Peak Practice and Liverpool-based soap Brookside as well as performing in West End musicals. Bours, a single mother to Millie, 11, and Lainie, nine, has now "retired from showbusiness" to concentrate on politics. Her job will be to rebut Labour claims that Ukip wants to privatise the NHS.

Jill Seymour, West Midlands MEP, Transport: the 54-year-old has held numerous roles in the party since joining 12 years ago. She is against positive discrimination legislation which allows boardroom's gender targets — something she compares to "vote fixing". Despite her many years in the party, she has stayed out of the media spotlight until now.

And an honourable mention for Suzanne Evans. Suzanne Evans Ukip's most high-profile former spokesman was ousted from her role after losing her seat as a councillor but will run for parliament in Shrewsbury. A Tory defector who has only been in the party for a year. She was rapidly appointed national communities spokesman. The former BBC reporter who now runs a PR agency, she has won plaudits within the party for her confidence in front of the camera. She blamed Ukip's poor performance in London (and the loss of her own seat) on "educated, cultured and young" in the capital who were less likely to vote for Ukip, and claimed the party was unlike the "metropolitan elite" in being able to understand the "heartache" felt by the rest of England.

There is much one could say about some of the colourful remarks by the aforementioned but, in the interests of time and economy, let's look at just one. The idea that "educated" and "cultured" and "young" people don't vote UKIP. It's really quite unusual for a politician to blame the electorate for not voting for them because said voters are "educated" and "cultured." The more sensitive — or perceptive — UKIP voter might feel a bit insulted; the inference being that a lack, if not an absence, of education and culture are prerequisites for voting UKIP.

Hey, Evans said it. I'm just putting it out there. Just saying, like.

Chapter 6:
Blankety Blank Cheque Book and Pen

*"It is a vast sum. I don't know what the total amount is but —
oh lor — it must be pushing £2 million"*
NIGEL FARAGE commenting on his expenses

UKIP's approach to policy differs considerably from that of
other parties in many ways. Not for them the focus groups,
researchers, economists and academics pressed into the
service of the cause to divine, to the absolute penny, what
the cost of implementing their program might be. There is
virtually no substantive explanation of what a UKIP government might cost the tax payer. A few vague references
to what leaving the EU might save the UK and that's about
your lot. Presumably the pounds and pence will be
addressed in the forthcoming manifesto. Ahem.

Policy, though, is only one area where the party's
unorthodox approach to cold hard cash manifests itself.
There is also the behaviour of the party's individual representatives to consider.

Given the strident protests UKIP issued in the wake of
the Westminster expenses scandal one would, reasonably,
assume that UKIP MEPs, at least, were paragons of ethical
accounting and above the sort of grubby, piss-taking greed
of the MPs who virtually rode the Westminster gravy train
into the ground. Well, not *quite...*

Neil Hamilton, the former Tory MP who, not to overstate the case, has a certain *history* in matters of this
nature, was the subject of an article in this regard by
Michael Crick for Channel 4's website on December 10th,
2014. Crick wrote: "Tonight, as Ukip is holding its selection meeting for the constituency of Basildon South, a

letter from the Ukip finance committee querying expenses claims made by the former Tory MP Neil Hamilton has been seen by Channel 4 News."

Hamilton was scheduled to attend a party selection meeting in Basildon to address party members' concerns about his ambitions to represent UKIP in one of its most high-profile constituencies. He'd previously been blocked from standing as a MEP and from the selection process in Boston and Skegness.

The former Tory was furious that the letter had been leaked and claimed he was the victim of jealousy and dirty tricks and a deliberate attempt on the part of his enemies to confuse matters, given, he claimed, that he'd already answered the questions included in the letter. Nevertheless, the letter was pretty incendiary stuff. In full, it read:

Dear Neil Hamilton,

To assist you in focusing your mind on Ukip's simple and not unreasonable request that you explain your expenses claims. Would you please provide details of the following to the F&RC Committee;

1. *In the case of each and every mileage claim, detail where you went, who you saw and why you had to make this trip.*

2. *Provide the invoice for each disbursement that you say you have incurred, detailing why this disbursement was incurred, and in the case of a lunch for example, whom you were having lunch with and for what purpose.*

3. *Provide an explanation of each stay that has been charged for your wife's flat detailing why it was more convenient for you to stay there, rather than at your house.*

4. *State who agreed that you were able to charge for staying in your wife's flat post the European elections.*

5. *Prior to the European elections, please confirm who agreed that you would be able to charge for your stay in your wife's flat, and obviously at the same time set out why, and where you were that required that you utilise this flat on a specific day. — More particularly what interested the committee is why, after you were removed from*

the job that you were originally allocated prior to the European elections, you continued to use this flat as you were no longer performing that role.

6. *To assist you, [Redacted] has specifically told us that he did not agree for you to charge VAT on the salary you received prior to the European Election. We have seen the email trail and would like an explanation as to why you did not go back to those who agreed this salary and why you did not make it known that you intended to charge VAT on your salary by charging Ukip through a company for your services as this incurred Ukip in extra costs. It is accepted that Ukip would have had to pay employer's NI which is substantially less than VAT. — What is wrong here, is that you failed to go back to the management committee to clear the arrangement knowing that Ukip was at all times during this campaign short of money.*

7. *To further assist you, in respect of expenses claimed with your new role, (Deputy Chairman Regions) [Redacted] has specifically told us that you could claim expenses for any tasks that he requested you to carry out. Accordingly can you please provide, for each item of work, confirmation that this was specifically done at [Redacted]'s behest.*

8. *We note that you have withdrawn your claim for attendance and stay at the Doncaster Conference as you now say that it was wrongly put in due to a "fit of pique" — whatever that means.*

9. *We further note that you are no longer proceeding with this claim at all. We find this somewhat surprising particularly as, if the expenses can be substantiated, as set out above, there is no reason for Ukip not to pay it or for you to withdraw the claim!*

10. *We need to place on record that we knew nothing of any expense claims you had put into Ukip until [Redacted] brought the expense claim that you have now withdrawn to my attention because [Redacted] had been asked on a couple of occasions by your wife to pay this invoice and [Redacted] felt that we ought to see it to confirm that payment was in order. In addition, prior to this, the NEC had asked for greater information to be provided to them on Ukip's finances and expenses and no doubt this is what prompted [Redacted] to mention this to us as he was concerned by it.*

11. *We hope the above will assist you in providing the information that is required to substantiate your claims. You have already had over a month to assemble this information and the F& RC committee should be obliged to receive this information by close of business Friday 19th December, particularly, as [Redacted] has pointed out to us, Ukip's year end is 31st December.*

12. *Please do bear in mind that we receive at Lexdrum House handwritten letters from pensioners enclosing a £5 or a £10 note which they have managed to save so as to send it to Ukip and hence we need to make sure that all expenses are fully explainable.*

Hamilton had ignited a storm of controversy as a Conservative MP when allegations that he took bungs — cash money in the infamous brown paper bags — as payment for asking questions in parliament on behalf of commercial interests. The former Tory had always denied the claims but they effectively halted his career as a Conservative politician.

Still, a chap deserves the benefit of the doubt and is innocent until proven guilty etc. How about the rest of 'em, you wonder? *The Mirror's* Ben Glaze was robust in his view, on January 12th, 2014, with the headline above his report reading: "UKIP leader Nigel Farage and Euro MPs pocket £800k in expenses — despite wanting UK to leave."

Glaze wrote: "His party want out of the EU but that isn't keeping them off the Brussels expenses gravy train. UKIP leader Nigel Farage and his Euro MPs claimed nearly £800,000 in expenses and allowances from the EU in one year while campaigning for Britain to leave." The journalist claimed UKIP's "grasping MEPs" had stuck the taxpayers with a bill for £370,000 for "office costs" and had claimed a further £420,000 for food and accommodation.

Other revelations included "MEP and deputy party leader Paul Nuttall" who had "employed 12 members of staff at public expense." Nuttall, it should be noted, has consistently maintained the worst attendance record of any MEP of any party in any country.

Farage and Midlands MEP Roger Helmer came in for a kicking too from Glaze as he revealed that both men employed their respective spouses who were on the "Brussels payroll." Farage's wife pocketed around £30K per year while Mrs. Helmer struggled heroically along on a paltry £20,000 per year. Glaze quoted an unnamed source who said: "Farage makes a big thing of pretending UKIP are different from other parties. But this shows they're even worse."

The *Sunday Mirror* claimed they'd accessed documents which revealed "UKIP MEPs claimed an average of £35,635 each in 'general expenditure allowances' in 2012."

It was all pretty interesting stuff. The party's implacable hostility to the EU was no bar to its MEPs raking in as much as they could from the hated institution. Of course all this was on top of their MEPs salary, which currently stands at £79,000 per annum. In addition there was first class travel expenses and the "daily subsistence allowance" to sweeten the pot.

Nuttall, North West MEP, who as we've seen has an attendance record best described as appalling, "claimed the daily subsistence allowance just 30 times in 2012" wrote Glaze. And "... donated £12,400 to UKIP since election in 2009, according to the Electoral Commission. His allowances claims last year ran to £40,436. He was among seven MEPs who gave UKIP a total of £425,978 in cash and other benefits after election."

Glaze went on to name the other UKIP passengers on the Brussels Gravy Express. They were: "Derek Clark, East Midlands, £56,822 general and subsistence allowances, £187,000 party donations since 2004; Stuart Agnew, East of England, £78,486 allowances, £31,000 donations since 2009; Mike Nattrass, West Midlands, £59,845 allowances, £96,000 donations since 2004, resigned in September; Godfrey Bloom, Yorkshire and Humber, £46,722 allowances, £72,000 donations since 2004."

In addition to the aforementioned Glaze included "MEPs who made no donations but claimed allowances." These were: "Gerard Batten, London, £51,977; John Bufton, Wales, £49,550; William Legge, South West, £53,813 and Roger Helmer, East Midlands, £67,410."

Glaze was pointed in his examination of Farage's Euro expenses, which were £61,065 but "... only includes subsistence for the last six months. In 2009, he said his MEPs would 'provide a quarterly expenses statement'. We found they have not published any for more than a year." Glaze continued: "Campaign group European Movement UK said: 'UKIP's position is hypocritical.'"

Of course UKIP defended the practice of its MEPs pointing out that they were only doing what every other MEP did and claiming only that to which they were entitled. Justifying Mrs. Farage picking up a wedge of Euros a UKIP spokesperson said: "Our MEPs claim allowances like other MEPs. Mr Farage employs his wife because his office is in his home for which he doesn't charge the taxpayer." How considerate.

Even the *Telegraph*, not a journal famed for its radical Marxism, felt compelled to note, on April 15th, 2014, that: "Farage could face investigation into EU expenses. A former senior Ukip official has filed a formal complaint about Mr Farage to the EU anti-fraud office OLAF." Apparently, there was a question regarding £60,000 of EU funds which had been paid into his personal account but which had gone "missing." The newspaper noted that the UKIP MEP had bagged around £16,000 every year since 2009 to pay "for the upkeep of his constituency office, a small converted grain store near Bognor Regis, West Sussex, according to transparency reports filed on the party's website."

The *Telegraph* reported that Farage's office premises had been made available to him, *rent free,* by UKIPers fifteen years previously. Not an unreasonable question, then, to wonder where the £16K had gone... *The Times* reckoned that "utilities and other non-rental costs amount to no more than £3,000 a year, according to the former office manager, leaving about £12,000 a year unexplained." UKIP, naturally, defended its man: "Nigel Farage is confident that he has abided by European parliamentary rules at all times when spending allowances. The Lyminster office is not the sole address that incurs expenditure in the pursuance of Mr Farage's job as an MEP, though it is the most important one."

Lawyers are touchy creatures so it's best to state the obvious; all the above might show greedy, hypocritical and thoroughly distasteful practice but there is no suggestion on the part of this author that UKIPers are engaged in criminal practice. Apart from Tom Wise, that is. The former UKIP MEP, according to the *Telegraph's* John Bingham, on November 11th, 2009, "... boasted openly about 'repatriating' money from the EU to Britain as he lodged his £3,000-a-month claims for office staff, a court heard. But, paying his researcher only a fraction of the allowance, he funnelled the rest into a secret bank account used to pay for shipments of fine wines and other personal expenditure."*

It was alleged, at Southwark Crown Court, that the one-time East of England MEP could have trousered nearly £180,000. Apparently, the crafty UKIPer had lied to EU officials and successfully blagged his way out of an investigation into allegations of "wrongdoing." Eventually he came clean, holding his hand up to the fraud and half-way through the trial for false accounting decided to change his plea to guilty, before his old boss, Nigel Farage, was called to give evidence against him.

The beak, Judge Geoffrey Rivlin QC, said that Wise was guilty of a "gross breach of trust" before continuing "It is no exaggeration to say that you had hardly got your feet beneath your desk as an MEP before you were planning to defraud the parliament to which you were elected and the people you were elected to serve. This was very deliberate and blatant dishonesty ... You knew the

In March 2015 it was revealed that Janice Atkinson MEP's assistant used the same word — repatriating – to try to fiddle hotel bills at the EU's expense.

system of expenses inside out and this was a claim you devised and planned with some care."

Bingham's *Telegraph* report continued:

> Wise, of Leighton Buzzard, Beds, was described in court as a "rising star" in the party who sat on the parliament's Culture, Media and Sport Committee. But he was forced to sit as an independent until the end of his term earlier this year after Ukip withdrew the whip.
>
> The court heard that Wise claimed £3,000 per month on his parliamentary "secretarial assistance allowance" but paid Mrs Jenkins, of Barons Court, west London, only £500. Although her signature appeared on the claims, it emerged that she was asked to sign blank documents which Wise would then complete. She was formally cleared of charges of false accounting and using criminal property after the disgraced politician's admission.
>
> A police investigation found that Wise spent £3,500 of taxpayers' money on 19 cases of fine wine — along with £1,000 of his own money. He also used £6,800 to clear his credit card bills, bought himself a second-hand Peugeot 206 with £6,400, and spent at least £1,200 on Ukip leaflets. But when the suspicious claims were investigated by the parliament's director general of finances he claimed that none of the money had been spent, other than Mrs Jenkins's salary and repaid more than £25,000. The judge noted: "This offence came to an end not because your conscience got the better of you, but only because your activities were exposed by the press, after which time you terminated the claim and repaid your ill-gotten gains in the hope of avoiding prosecution."
>
> Jonathan Fisher QC, defending, said the revelations had been "truly catastrophic" for his client, leaving his "reputation and integrity in tatters". "The pathos of his plight is palpable for all to feel and to see," he said.

Bless.

Ashley Mote, though, was the UKIPer that ensured Wise was only following precedent. Mr. Mote, not an MP but an MEP, thus not entitled to be addressed as 'honourable', dealt his party a bit of a kick in the goolies in its fight against benefit scroungers and fraudsters when he copped a spell of porridge for, you guessed it, benefit fraud. The *Guardian,* from September 5th, 2007, laid out the tacky details: "A British member of the European parliament will continue to get £75,000 a year in salary and expenses despite being jailed yesterday for swindling £65,500 from the taxpayer in a five-year benefits fraud."

Mote had been elected in 2004 but was booted from UKIP following his charging with fraud; serving out his parliamentary term as an independent MEP aligning himself with a bloc of far-right MEPs. He got nine months which didn't actually exclude him from continuing as an MEP. According to EU rules an MEP would need to receive a sentence of a year before expulsion from the Parliament would ensue. During his time in stir the disgraced fraudster would continue to draw his £79,000 annual salary and, even more bizarrely, his £1,200 monthly allowance for office expenses!

The *Guardian* reported that Mote was a member of the parliament's Budgetary Control Committee, which must've been a nice gig for someone of his proclivities. And that Portsmouth Crown Court was where he'd been convicted of twenty-one separate offences. The Judge, though, seemed sympathetic. Richard Price said: "To say that this case has ruined you is an understatement; it is a tragedy. You have worked amazingly hard as an MEP. But only a custodial sentence would be appropriate." You have to feel for the man, right?

The *Guardian* report concluded: "The court heard that Mote's public relations company collapsed in 1990. He then claimed housing and council tax benefits between 1991 and 1993 before finding freelance work in 1995. He claimed benefits again from 1996 but failed to declare income from various enterprises. Ukip leader Nigel Farage called on Mote to resign his seat if he had "a shred of decency or integrity left".

So OK; maybe UKIPers are as greedy and as grasping as the next on-the-make politico but as the only party combating the 'Westminster Elite' they're still on the side of the little guy, right? They're going to crack down hard on, say, tax dodgers and avoiders, yes? They're out to make sure the tax payer isn't unnecessarily put upon by the 'elite'? Well, not exactly... February, 12th, 2015 saw eleven of UKIP's MEPs line up alongside Greek's fascists, Golden Dawn, and vote *against* a proposition designed to clamp down on tax-dodging. The other twelve elected UKIP MEPs, including Nigel Farage were, one can only assume, busy as they didn't bother to turn up at all.

Sadly, for our would-be champions of the little people, the motion was passed by 612 votes to 19. The proposal intended to deal rigorously with tax-dodgers was supported by all the main pro-EU outfits and even some of the hard right ones, including France's *Front National.* UKIP's constant protestations that it isn't a far right or extremist party were, presumably, left intact despite siding with Golden Dawn.

It was certainly an interesting move by UKIP when one considers the press release issued by party officials the day after their efforts to thwart moves against tax-dodging came to naught. The statement read: "We believe that tax evasion by individuals should face a zero tolerance approach. Every pound that one person manages to illegally evade equates to an extra pound that a law-abiding taxpayer has to pay." And: "Britain's three corporate political parties should hang their heads in shame that they have all proven so lax and so lenient towards tax evaders while hammering working people on modest incomes with hefty tax bill"s." There was more: "Britain needs a party that does not turn a blind eye to those who seek to dodge what they are legally bound to pay while still availing themselves of the many advantages of living or doing business in Britain. UKIP is the one party with the appetite to tackle these infuriating abuses."

By now the reader will be acquainted with that age-old political tactic — that of saying one thing while doing quite the other — there is little doubt that UKIP is now among its finest and most-skilled practitioners. None of which stopped Farage's shameless efforts to justify his party's hypocrisy and decision to vote against the measures. According to Nigel things weren't that simple.

According to him "straightforward" tax avoidance wasn't especially "bad" or even "wrong." Of course, the reader will understand perfectly well the subtle distinction that exists between tax dodging (or evasion) which is illegal and tax avoidance which isn't illegal. However, this is hardly the point; which remains that business and the rich continue to deploy means denied to the rest of the population to reduce their tax liability and, as a consequence, pay a lower percentage of their 'earnings' than those at the bottom of the earnings league.

It wouldn't be unfair if the reader were to doubt UKIP's claims that, somehow, it is an 'anti-establishment' party, intent on tackling the 'Westminster elite' on behalf of ordinary Joe and Joan Soap.

Chapter 7:
Gay Donkey
Raped my Horse

"Some homosexuals prefer sex with animals"
former UKIPer **Julia Gasper**

By now the reader will have gained at least some insight into the mindset and character of the average UKIPer and the sorts of things that might happen to the UK if the party got its hands on the levers of power. There are many descriptions one might wish to use in an attempt to accurately portray UKIP but it's unlikely that 'politically correct' would ever be one of them. Nevertheless that's exactly the formulation favoured by Godfrey William Bloom as he grumpily exited the party. The reader will already be acquainted, at least in passing, with Bloom by now. It's worth looking a little closer at him, though, given his not inconsiderable contribution to UKIP.

Described by the Plain English Campaign as "a wince-inducing gaffe machine" he represented Yorkshire and the Humber for UKIP in the European Parliament for nine years, from 2004 to 2013. In September of 2013 he lost the party whip and saw out his electoral term as an independent, eventually resigning from UKIP in October 2014.

Bloom's observations on everything from women to foreign aid are the stuff of near-legend and, despite his personal friendship with Farage, his public utterances have been extremely unhelpful to the UKIP leader as he struggled to rid the party of its extremist image.

During his stint in the European Parliament, Bloom served on the Committee for Women's Rights and Gender Equality. An office, it often seemed, he never quite understood, as his forthright opinions on the matter seemed to indicate. For example, just a few weeks into his appointment, he announced that "no self-respecting small businessman with a brain in the right place would ever employ a lady of child-bearing age." Other gems included: "I am here to represent Yorkshire women who always have dinner on the table when you get home." On the question of prostitution Bloom talked of "terrified young women beaten into prostitution, often from Eastern Europe" before comprehensively destroying any perceived sensitivity and empathy on his part by concluding, "In short, most girls do it because they want to."

In 2004 he extended an invitation to Cambridge University's women's rugby club to visit the European Parliament buildings. It didn't go well. The visit ended in Bloom being accused of sexual assault, which he denied, and of making "sexist and misogynistic" remarks.

Further demonstrating his unique understanding of the work of the committee to which he'd been appointed, he asserted that feminism was a "passing fashion" made up by "shrill, bored, middle-class women of a certain physical genre" and that men sympathetic to feminism were "...the slightly effete politically-correct chaps who get sand kicked in their face on the beach." In case anyone missed his point he pointed out that women were more skilled in the art of "... finding the mustard in the pantry" than driving cars.

It would be unfair to Bloom to suggest his intellect and penetrating insight were confined solely to the areas of women's rights and gender equality. Not so. On the matter of climate change: "As far as I am concerned man-made global warming is nothing more than a hypothesis that hasn't got any basis in fact." On the bombing of the Rainbow Warrior: "Here we have one of the most truly fascist boats since 1945, well done the French for sinking it."

In an interview with LBC Radio in November, 2013, Bloom demanded that the right to vote be withdrawn from the unemployed and public sector workers before demonstrating that he might well be Godfrey Bloom but he isn't always wrong when he described David Cameron as "pigeon-chested; the sort of chap I used to beat up."

Arguably, Bloom's most infamous declaration, however, was on the question of foreign aid. As Rowena Mason reported for the *Guardian*, on August 7th, 2013, "A senior UKIP politician has been recorded telling activists that Britain should not be sending aid to 'Bongo Bongo land.' At a meeting of UKIP members in the West Midlands the 'wince-inducing gaffe machine' produced the epitaph which would underline an extraordinary political career.

Rubbishing the foreign aid budget as something that would only be squandered by its recipients on 'Ray-Ban sunglasses' and 'apartments in Paris', Bloom left witnesses stunned. He asked the meeting in Stourbridge, 'How we can possibly be giving a billion pounds a month when we're in this sort of debt to Bongo Bongo land is completely beyond me. To buy Ray-Ban sunglasses, apartments in Paris, Ferraris and all the rest of it that goes with most of the foreign aid. F18s for Pakistan. We need a new squadron of F18s. Who's got the squadrons? Pakistan, where we send the money.'"

With his customary disregard for timing, tact and strategy, Bloom brought his party bosses to a near-nervous breakdown when he made his remarks — which, of course, would've been bad enough at any time — in the same week that his party was to publish the names of its approved candidates for the following year's Euro elections.

Immediately another storm erupted over UKIP's racism and intolerance, with several MPs demanding Farage discipline the blundering Bloom and/or ban him from standing for election as a UKIP candidate. Failure to do so, it was suggested, would both ensure UKIP's racist credentials and its hypocrisy; given that just scant weeks previously Farage had been key to the expulsion of an Italian MEP from UKIP's European caucus for remarks about one of his country's Ministers; who, the Italian, suggested was a member of the "government of Bongo Bongo" whose aim was to introduce "tribal traditions" and who would better serve his country by leaving politics and seeking employment as a housekeeper.

Bloom was typically *blasé,* laughing off the accusation that his remarks were racist as "absurd" and "laughable" and stated bluntly, "What's wrong with that? I'm not a wishy-washy Tory. I don't do political correctness ... The fact that the *Guardian* is reporting this will probably double my vote in the north of England." The *Guardian* reported further Bloom bombshells from the Stourbridge meeting: "You can torture people to death but you jolly well can't give them a full life sentence because that's against their human rights."

"We can't hang them because we're now a member of the European Union and it's embedded in the treaty of Rome. It's a personal thing but I'd hang the bastards myself ... Especially for some of these, especially for the guy who hacked the soldier to death. I do hope they would ask me to throw the rope over the beam because I'd be delighted to do so."

Unsurprisingly, his remarks were not greeted with equanimity from all quarters. Labour's Shadow Development Minister, Rushanara Ali, commented, "It's just offensive and the kind of thing that should have been consigned to the history books. It's completely at odds with the 21st century. If Nigel Farage is serious about getting rid of racism and intolerance in his party, he should take action against politicians who think it's acceptable to speak of people in developing countries in that way."

John Mann, Labour MP for Bassetlaw, insisted UKIP "throw him out and stop him standing as an MEP".

One could continue. There is more. Much more but the point is clear; Bloom is UKIP man made flesh. The concentrated essence, if you like. Eventually, however, the incessant 'political correctness' all got too much for poor old Godfrey and *The Independent* carried the news of his departure on October 13th, 2014: 'The former Ukip MEP who called women 'sluts' and complained about aid being sent to 'Bongo Bongo Land' has quit the party because it is becoming too 'politically correct'."

Prior to his resignation Bloom had been banned by his party from speaking, publicly, at any official UKIP events; a move that had incensed the bellicose right-winger. On announcing his resignation he advised UKIP's newly-minted and first MP, Douglas Carswell to "watch his back."

Bitterly, Bloom railed against his former colleagues, complaining live on LBC Radio that, "UKIP were supposed to be something new, but now we seem to be drifting towards the political correct mainstream just like everyone else and that's not the reason people voted Ukip. Instead of it being the libertarian party of common sense, I've been banned from speaking. I don't know where the party has gone astray, but it seems to have gone astray."

It's improbable that Bloom is the only person who has concerns about UKIP's direction and evolution. Certainly, the party's candidate for the seat of Cardiff South and Penarth, John Rees-Evans, seems to share some of Godfrey's concerns. Under the surreal headline, "Gay donkey rapists and other oddities" the *Guardian* reported on December 22nd, 2014 that its Chair, Steve Crowther, had recently urged party members not to express what might be considered "odd" views on social media.

The advice was prompted by a YouTube video, courtesy of UKIP's candidate for Cardiff South and Penarth, John Rees-Evans, which had led to the truly collectable head-line, 'Gay Donkey Tried To Rape My Horse.' According to the *Guardian* Rees-Evans had become involved in an altercation with anti-UKIP demonstrators outside the party's new premises in Merthyr Tydfil. It seemed that Rees-Evans had been needled over some of the more out-rageous observations of his party colleagues. The tipping point being Julia Gasper's bonkers assertion that some homosexuals preferred sex with animals. The *Guardian* quoted the blundering Rees-Evans responding thus: "Actually, I've witnessed that. I was personally quite amazed. I've got a horse and it was there in the field. And a donkey came up, which was male, and I'm afraid tried to rape my horse." By his distorted reasoning Gasper's statement was "obviously correct" because a gay donkey had clearly fancied Rees-Evans' horse.

If, at this point, you simply can't get your head around what you're reading spare a thought for this writer...

The UKIPer told the *Guardian* "It is not as though I was making a serious point. I was simply answering a question, rather than telling the person that he was ridiculous for raising it. I was asked to respond to quite a bizarre statement, and it's my view that British people are fed up with politicians evading uncomfortable questions and so I tried to give the only kind of answer I knew how to give because, frankly, I do not have any experience of homosexuality, or humans copulating with animals. So the closest match, from my personal experience, was the case of what appeared to be homosexuality with animals."

Rees-Evans is the stuff of which party chief's nightmares are made. His explanation for the staggering number of howlers emanating from his colleagues is that "The reality is that, when you have a party that does not have a whipping system, where politicians fear being disciplined for saying the wrong thing, inevitably you will have quite a diversity of personal opinion." Or, alternatively, that if your party is glued together by racism, bigotry, homophobia and intolerance it will attract racists, bigots, homophobes and the intolerant. With such a membership, then, such utterances will become the norm rather than the exception.

Rees-Evans concluded, "Ukip is essentially at a crossroads, in the sense that it can go two ways. It can either say look, sadly, you guys are going to have to shut up and avoid answering questions, or crack on, answer questions honestly. We will occasionally get into trouble but we would prefer to have that kind of libertarian ethos in the party that allows you to say whatever you think." Despite all this, or maybe even because of it, as UKIP would probably contend, the party has continued to grow and attract support. Today it has two MPs, three members of the House of Lords and twenty-four Members of the European Parliament (MEPs). It is now the UK's largest party in the European Parliament and claims a membership of around 40,000 which, possibly, makes it bigger than the Liberal Democrats. UKIP has come a long way since it's one-time leadership contender and then highest-profile member, the perma-tanned chat-show host, Robert Kilroy-Silk flounced out of the party to form Veritas, describing UKIP, as he went, as "a joke."

The breakthrough year was 2013 when the local elections saw the party achieve its biggest successes thus far. It won a twenty-three percent average share of the vote and won 147 seats. Norfolk, Lincolnshire and Kent were the strongest areas for the party with gains of fifteen, sixteen and seventeen seats respectively. The polls around that time consistently placed UKIP third with nationwide support around the eighteen percent mark.

Continuing its upward trajectory, 2014 was the party's most successful year so far. The European Elections of that year saw the party trounce its rivals by considerable margins. It gained more votes than any other British party, nearly twenty-eight percent of the total votes cast, and won a further eleven seats to take its total to twenty-four. Worryingly, for Cameron and Miliband, UKIP proved its ability to steal votes from both the Conservatives and Labour when the results showed that the party had won seats in every region; even in Scotland — albeit only one — where the party is generally considered to be toxic.

The autumn of 2014 iced UKIP's cake with the party finally securing its first Westminster seats. Both the winning candidates were Tory defectors who recorded impressive swings to overturn their previous Conservative majorities.

The first was Douglas Carswell who, on October 9th, took Clacton by 12,404 votes. This represented nearly a sixty percent share of the vote and a swing of forty-four percent from the Conservatives to UKIP. Described by *The Economist* as "The thinking man's UKIPer", Carswell was the *Telegraph's* Briton of the Year in 2009 and *The Spectator's* readership voted him Parliamentarian of the Year in the same year. As a Tory MP he was also involved in the Westminster expenses scandal. In 2005, following his election, he recorded his one million-pound London flat as his second home and claimed over £20,000 for food, furniture and running costs. Then, in 2007, he designated his house in Thorpe-le-Soken as his second home. A practice known as 'flipping.' Carswell paid the deposit, purchased furniture, including the famous love seat for nearly seven hundred pounds, and then claimed the cash back on his expenses. Over the following two years he blagged an extra £32,000 in expenses against household expenditure and in the financial year ending in 2013 claimed just shy of forty grand which was more than any other Essex MP. Because he's worth it.

A barrister and economist, Mark Reckless is a bit different in that he barely had time to get his feet under the Conservative benches before eloping with UKIP. Entering parliament for the first at the 2010 General Election, representing Rochester and Strood, he served just four years before resigning from the Tories, resigning his seat and then fighting the resulting by-election under UKIP colours.

A month after Carswell's election Reckless gave UKIP its second MP when he won his old seat with a forty-two percent share of the vote; comfortably trouncing his old party who polled 34.8 percent (the Lib Dems endured the greater humiliation, losing their deposit with just 0.87 percent share of the vote).

It's unlikely that UKIP has peaked and despite a slight dip in the polls in early 2015 — suggesting the party has around nine percent support; below ten percent for the first time in months — most pollsters agree that the party is on course to secure around half-a-dozen seats in the 2015 general election.

Victoria Ayling has been mentioned in previous chapters, of course, but an article in *The Independent*, on February 22nd, 2015, about her campaign in Grimsby, contained the now-familiar themes of resentful voters, taken for granted and abused by the three main parties. Areas where UKIP's populist presentation could do the Conservatives and Labour significant damage. Jamie Merrill reported: "Handing out purple leaflets and dressed head to toe in purple, Victoria Ayling looks every inch the Ukip candidate. But she's not chasing Tory votes in Essex and Kent; she has her sights set at Labour in its once safe seat of Great Grimsby in Lincolnshire. Commentators and pollsters have identified the constituency as a key target in the general election. Most of the attention has focused on Nigel Farage in South Thanet, but it's here in the North, where the party is seeking to win Labour votes, that Ukip has one of the best chances of winning."

Merrill's article was an in-depth look at the constituency and some of the problems its residents faced and, of course, Ayling's response. One of which was the decline of the town's fishing industry which, one can safely assume, is to be blamed on the European Union.

According to Merrill, while Ayling received a mixed response from the constituency's electorate it was far from unsympathetic with one pensioner, Doreen Campbell, 79, quoted as saying, "This town is like a sinking ship with old politicians running an old town and I'm worried about the same thing as everyone else in this town — and that's the Poles." Another, David Gowen, 83, writes Merrill, "... has lived here all his life, grabs her [Ayling's] arm to say that's he an admirer of 'Nigel', and like many of his friends he used to vote Labour, but he's 'flipping angry' with the 'current lot' in Westminster, who 'only care about themselves' and have let 'too many foreigners in'."

Despite being almost a template for a rock-solid safe Labour seat the pollsters present worrying findings for Miliband and his strategists. Merrill references a Lord Ashcroft poll which indicates that "Ukip makes up 34 per cent of the vote, just 1 per cent behind Labour. For her part, Ms Ayling is clearly popular, she came within 700 votes of winning the seat for the Conservative party in 2010 before defecting to the anti-European Union party. "I might originally be from south London," says Ms Ayling, who has previously been recorded saying "send the lot back" in reference to immigrants, "But I've lived and worked around Grimsby for decades and we are quite literally at the end of the line up here, and people are suffering. We need to shake things up and get out of Europe."

Merrill shrewdly identifies the seeming paradoxes of UKIP's popularity in such an area. On the one had, in contrast to most of the rest of the county, the constituency has seen very little immigration. One of UKIP's familiar refrains, that immigrants are stealing British jobs, would be ineffective; there are no jobs to steal and virtually no immigrants to steal them if there were (Merrill says the last census recorded the area as 96% white British). On the other hand, the factors identified earlier by Robert Ford and Matthew Goodwin, in their book *Revolt on the Right*, clearly come into play. As Merrill notes, "What the town is though, is old, working-class and poorly educated."

Other factors which make the seat vulnerable to a UKIP assault are youth unemployment at 25% and a stagnating population. Virtually begging UKIP to take the seat is the Labour Party whose retiring MP, Austin Mitchell, displayed the sort of arrogance, complacency and contempt for its voters that many feel is now a

Labour trademark. Boasting to *The Independent on Sunday*, Mitchell said that Labour would retain its seat even if it stood a "raving alcoholic sex paedophile." Such appalling smugness plays right into UKIP's hands and Ayling wasted no time in making the expected political capital, stating that "It's insulting to the great people of Great Grimsby and it's exactly the sort of 'take them for granted' attitude that is turning people away from the establishment parties." Quite. Mitchell's arrogance plays straight to UKIP's outsider posturing and the righteous indignation garnered by Ayling might yet hit Labour where it hurts most; right in the ballot box.

Labour, it seems, just will not get the message and one can only imagine the whoops of glee UKIP staffers emitted on learning of Mitchell's remarks. Frequently, in politics, perception is reality and the medium is the message. It appears UKIP is learning this very quickly while Labour is doing its best to forget it.

Chapter 8:
It's Just a Jump
to the Left...

"... people talk about UKIP being bigots. There are hundreds of thousands of bigots in the United Kingdom and they deserve representation."
UKIP Party Secretary **Matthew Richardson**

In 2010, Farage was re-elected as UKIP leader for a second stretch. Today, Farage-led UKIP, while keeping Europe at the heart of its orientation, has broadened its policy-base and the party's official website provides — at last! — a little insight into what UKIP represents today. Under the heading, *What We Stand For*, UKIP outlines its mission statement:

— *UKIP is a patriotic party that promotes independence: from the EU, and from government interference. We believe in free trade, lower taxes, personal freedom and responsibility.*

— *UKIP believes in Britain becoming a democratic, self-governing country once again. This can only be achieved by getting our nation out of the European Union and reasserting the sovereignty of Parliament.*

— *As a party we are unashamedly patriotic: we believe there is so much to be proud about Britain and the contribution it has made to the world. We believe that Britain is good enough to be an independent nation, trading and building harmonious relations with the rest of the world.*

— *We believe Britain must get back control over its borders, so that it can welcome people with a positive contribution to make while limiting the overall numbers of migrants and keeping out those without the skills or aptitudes to be of benefit to the nation.*

— UKIP believes in promoting self-reliance and personal freedom from state interference. We believe the state in Britain has become too large, too expensive and too dominant over civil society.

Return Power to the UK

- A vote for UKIP is a vote to leave the EU and recover power over our national life.

- Free trade, but not political union, with our European neighbours. We are the EU's largest export market: they depend on us for jobs — not the other way around.

- Binding local and national referenda, at the public's request, on major issues.

Protect Our Borders

- Regain control of our borders and of immigration — only possible by leaving the EU.

- Immigrants must financially support themselves and their dependents for 5 years. This means private health insurance (except emergency medical care), private education and private housing — they should pay into the pot before they take out of it.

- A points-based visa system and time-limited work permits.

- Proof of private health insurance must be a precondition for immigrants and tourists to enter the UK.

Rebuild Prosperity

- Save £55m a day in membership fees by leaving the EU and give British workers first crack at the 800,000 jobs we currently advertise to EU workers.

- No tax on the minimum wage.

- Enrol unemployed welfare claimants onto community schemes or retraining workfare programmes.

- Scrap HS2, all green taxes and wind turbine subsidies.

- Develop shale gas to reduce energy bills and free us from dependence on foreign oil and gas — place the tax revenues into a British Sovereign Wealth Fund.

- UKIP will abolish inheritance tax. Inheritance tax brings in under £4bn — less than a third of what we spend on *foreign aid. The super-rich avoid it, while modest property owners get caught by it. It hits people during a time of grief and UKIP will budget in its 2015 spending plans to completely abolish this unfair death tax.*

● *Make cuts to foreign aid that are real and rigorous.*

Safeguard Against Crime All

● *No cuts to front line policing.*

● *Make sentences mean what they say.*

● *No votes for prisoners — that's what losing your liberty means.*

● *Prevent foreign criminals entering the UK — by re-introducing border controls that the EU forced us to abandon.*

● *Scrap the European Arrest Warrant, which sends British citizens to foreign jails without evidence, just to answer questions — replace it with a proper extradition system.*

● *Remove the UK from the jurisdiction of the European Court of Human Rights.*

Care And Support For All

● *Open GP surgeries in the evening, for full-time workers, where there is demand.*

● *Locally-elected County Health Boards to inspect hospitals — to avoid another Stafford Hospital crisis.*

● *Prioritise social housing for people whose parents and grandparents were born locally.*

● *Allow the creation of new grammar schools.*

● *Make welfare a safety net for the needy, not a bed for the lazy. Benefits only available to those who have lived here for over 5 years.*

Free Speech and Democracy

● *No to Political Correctness — it stifles free speech.*

● *The law of the land must apply to us all. We oppose any other system of law.*

● *Teach children positive messages and pride in their country. We want to unite through better integration.*

All of this clearly defines UKIP as a pro-capitalist, anti-state, anti-immigrant, right-libertarian formation. The above outlines the party's traditional hostility to the EU, characterised by that curious blend of xenophobia and paranoia common among the far-right, seasoned by the arrogance of the jingoist. It's doubtful, for example, that the German economy could ever be said to "depend on us for jobs."

The paradoxes are stark, though. As David Osler noted in chapter four, it's an odd sort of libertarian party that would adopt UKIP's stance on borders and immigration.

Sadly, despite Farage's efforts to paint UKIP as the friend of the common people none of the above will benefit the British working class in any meaningful sense. There is a very weak argument that immigrants undercutting the minimum wage are responsible for driving down British wages but UKIP's uncritical worship of business deliberately ignores a vital point; British bosses paying under the minimum wage are breaking the law. Why no measures to deal with these law-breakers? Why not lift some of the legal shackles from trade unions so that they may more effectively organise immigrant workers and ensure they are earning no less than other workers, thus — by UKIP logic — protecting British workers' jobs?

Besides, capital can leap from one side of the world to the other at the stroke of a banker's keyboard so why shouldn't workers have the same freedom to better themselves and their families? As for insisting on private health insurance before even tourists can visit the UK, one wonders how on earth that could do anything other than damage Britain's tourism industry.

Regarding the 800,000 jobs where to start with this? Firstly, it's somewhat dishonest to imply that British workers are somehow exempt from 800,000 jobs UKIP claims are available across Europe. They aren't. *Any* EU citizen can apply for these jobs and rightly so. Why should any one country's workers have a monopoly on these jobs? If, on the other hand, they aren't and UKIP are claiming that those 800,000 jobs are *British* jobs that are only available to other EU citizens, well, that's somewhat less than honest. There are barely 559,000 vacancies available and unemployment is officially 2 million as of Jan 21st 2015. That's without the usual government sleight-of-hand and massaging of figures. There are easily a further half million unemployed not represented in the official two million. Bottom line; there are far more unemployed people than there are jobs available. That's the *real* problem. Scapegoating other EU citizens and blaming immigrants can't disguise that fact.

No tax on the minimum wage? The amount of tax paid on forty hours earnings at the national minimum wage wouldn't cover the cost of Nigel's lunch. Why not increase the minimum wage to a *living* wage? To an amount that allows people to do more than just cling on by their fingertips to survive? If they're even that lucky. Freeing up income that can be spent on something other than servicing personal debt and the extortionate rents charged by rip-off landlords would do far more for the economy than UKIP's token nod towards the nation's *real* wealth-creators.

Abolishing inheritance tax benefits absolutely no one but the already well-off. Why doesn't UKIP, instead, propose measures for closing loopholes and collecting the estimated £89 billion per year in legally and illegally dodged, evaded and avoided corporation tax?

And as for making people work for dole money; well, if there is work available, and UKIP thinks there is as they insist the unemployed should be doing it, then why not pay them the going wage for doing so instead of giving them benefits? How can they justify paying less than the legal national minimum wage? How can they justify forcing people to work for less than that? Because, of course, it's all part of the kick the poor trip all the main parties have been on for years. A shot in the campaign to blame the poor for the crisis Nigel's mates in the City triggered in the first place. Apart from anything else we need to stop thinking of dole money as a benefit. It's paid for by national insurance contributions. It's an *entitlement*. How insulting that, for example, a fire-fighter is made redundant as a result of austerity cuts and is then told he or she needs to work for dole money after contributing twenty year's worth of national insurance contributions, as well as contributing an important life-saving service to the nation? Mind you, UKIP's views are similar to the Tories on this one.

The latest wheeze from UKIP's would-be proletarian defenders takes poor-bashing into some novel and interesting areas, as the *Guardian's* John Harris noted on January 23rd, 2015, "A Ukip parliamentary candidate named Lynton Yates this week suggested banning benefit claimants from driving: 'Why do they have the privilege to spend the tax payers [sic] hard-earned money on a car, when those in work are struggling to keep their own car on the road?' Ukip's communications people said that Yates's suggestions were 'not Ukip policies and they will not form part of the Ukip manifesto', and the media rejoiced in the week's example of the party's supposed fruitcakery — though at the time of writing, Mr Yates was still Ukip's choice for the East Midlands seat of Charnwood." Sadly, while Yates' suggestion ought to provoke outrage Harris noted that such suggestions are virtually main-stream these days.

Thirty years since Thatcher set in train the reversal of the post-war consensus, New Labour and the Conservatives have willingly conspired to finish the job. A crucial strand of the new class war is the demonising and stigmatising of benefit claimants, the disabled and working-poor. It's now dangerously close that a majority of the population view such people as barely deserving of anything other than the very minimum needed to actually stay alive.

It's certainly no exaggeration to suggest that such a philosophy is now institutionalised. The DWP, along with Labour-appointed Atos (and no doubt its successor, Maximus, even if it tidies away some of Atos's crasser failures) operates a policy of intimidation, sanctions and bullying. The default assumption is that anyone in need of benefits is a 'scrounger' deserving only exposure and punishment by loss of desperately-needed benefits. Benefits which, contrary to the reactionary myth of the unemployed living in luxury, thanks to taxpayers' largesse, are among the very lowest in the world and only serve to leave people mired in poverty.

Harris writes, "Which brings us to some of this week's most sobering revelations, in material just published by the House of Commons work and pensions committee relating to the government's use of so-called sanctions: the punishments that take the form of a sudden withdrawal of benefits for at least four weeks. Echoing Iain Duncan Smith, the Tory Employment minister Esther McVey explains the practice in terms of "ending the something-for-nothing culture". Whatever their department is trying to do has resulted in an explosion of sanctioning — up from a rate of about 1,000 cases a month 10 years ago to a recent peak of 12,000 — and incontrovertible evidence of nastiness and abuse."

Harris also noted that the Trussell Trust, the largest providers and administrators of the UK's rocketing food bank 'industry', reckon that "over 50% of referrals to food banks in 2013-2014 were a result of benefit delays or changes, including sanctions".

Harris's article is a superbly-written and starkly-presented exposé of the state of the nation. He goes on to highlight the effects of such a culture on the disabled, the mentally-ill and those simply unfortunate enough to lose their minimum wage-paying opportunity to live lives as modern slaves. The reader is urged to seek out the article in full but for now, Harris's conclusion makes for a welcome breath of reality amidst the poor-bashing and scape-goating of the UK's most desperate and vulnerable people: "Beyond questions of the sometimes difficult relationship between disability and paid work, three-quarters of JSA claimants sign off within six months, and our insecure job market means people bounce in and out of unemployment but a public encouraged to think of "the unemployed" and "welfare claimants" as some separate, degenerate Other seems barely to notice what is happening. In other words, there are millions of Lynton Yateses, happily complicit in the cruelties for which their taxes pay and presumably ready to cheer for more."

The unemployed-poor; the gainfully-employed poor — who, UKIP won't tell you, account for a larger share of the benefits bill than the unemployed, such is the appallingly low level of wages in the UK today that they are forced to rely on tax credits and other government-funded in-work benefits; immigrants; the disabled... are all targets for UKIP. The very people Nigel Farage would have us believe his party somehow champions in the face of the war waged against them by the 'establishment' and 'Westminster-elite'.

Still, Nigel is currently having the last laugh in this regard. As Jane Merrick reported for *The Independent* on December 14th, 2014 "Voters see Ukip as more left wing than the Conservative Party in a shock poll finding that will fuel concerns among Ed Miliband's allies that Nigel Farage is 'parking his tanks on Labour's lawn'. A poll for *The Independent on Sunday* exposes what Labour strategists have been fearing for months — that voters do not regard Ukip as a party of the far right, but as one closer to the centre ground than the Tories. As such it could win Labour votes in the North. It suggests that attempts by Labour to portray Mr Farage's party as 'more Thatcher-ite than Thatcher' have fallen flat."

It is perplexing, to say the least, that voters could consider UKIP to the left of the Conservatives but that is exactly what the ComRes poll suggested. As Merrick reported, "Voters were asked to locate themselves, political parties and leaders on a spectrum ranging from 0, very left wing, to 10, very right wing, with 5 at the centre. The average voter puts themselves at 5.26. Mr Miliband (4.11) and the Labour Party (4.13) are perceived to be closer to the average person than David Cameron (6.81) or the Conservative Party (6.91). Mr Farage, on 6.59, and Ukip, on 6.61, are to the left of the Prime Minister and the Tories" and that, "Fascinatingly, the Conservative Party is considered more right-wing by Conservative voters (7.11) than Ukip is by Ukip voters (6.28). Ukip voters see themselves as less right-wing (5.86) than Conservative voters see themselves (6.44)."

Despite its obvious and visible Toryism-on-steroids large sections of the electorate are *still* buying the idea that UKIP represents some sort of pro-working class outfit, committed to the cause of the toiling masses. Certainly the party has recently bolted-on a couple of things traditionally considered the preserve of the left but it wouldn't be unduly cynical to doubt the party's sincerity in these areas and its commitment to such policies. Nevertheless, UKIP is definitely gaining electoral traction among the traditional Labour-voting working class.

Publisher, Damian Hockney, former UKIP vice-chair, in an article for *Our Kingdom — Power and Liberty in Britain*, in April 2014, titled, *UKIP is Closer to the Left than Many Think* craftily makes no real attempt to position UKIP as a left-of-centre party, still a ludicrous undertaking, whatever one ComRes poll might suggest. Instead he argues that UKIP has transcended traditional political definitions of left and right, while offering enough common ground to share with disaffected traditionally 'left' voters. This might go some way to explaining the perception of UKIP by some working class voters. Hockney insists that "UKIP's status as a right wing party features anomalies that are too big to bury or ignore."

Of course, there is a very simple explanation and it is simply that UKIP is opportunistically exploring every possible avenue to widen its base of support. Unsurprisingly, Hockney disagrees, instead believing that UKIP cannot "...be rammed into some format to fit left/right of UK politics and that it cannot either now be so easily dismissed as BNP-lite."

Disingenuously Hockney offers up the consideration that UKIP cannot be adjudged to be a party of the right because some of its voters and supporters back policies traditionally considered the preserve of the left; renationalisation of rail, opposition to privatisation of the Royal Mail and utilities. Such arguments are pitifully thin. By his reasoning Labour must be a socialist party; after all it contains socialists and far more of its members would support such policies as those outlined above than UKIP's members and supporters. He states that "these awkward bits which do not fit the political jigsaw are ignored by almost all the media and commentators, who sit with pieces that do not fit the puzzle and bang them with some force into the wrong holes just for convenience."

Nevertheless, Hockney perceives, correctly, that UKIP is in a state of flux and that such changes open up hitherto unconsidered possibilities for the party based on the new-found "attraction of the party to many former voters of 'the left'. On the NEC in about 2004/2005 we began to realise that our days as 'The Tory Party in Mourning' could be celebrated as over and done. The fear 'you'll let Labour in' has now gone from most of the UKIP ranks. And one of the intriguing possibilities it reveals, without actually taking the point to its logical conclusion, is the fluctuating position of UKIP on the spectrum in regard to specific issues, and what elected UKIP MPs might do when faced with even just a handful of seats in a tricky parliamentary situation."

To be fair to Hockney he does attempt to back his contention with some provable examples: "... my colleague Hulme Cross refused to budge over his lone support for sacked workers on the fire authority, attracting pressure and ire not just from the Tories who had a kind of de facto majority on the body, but also from the rest of the establishment, left and right. On the police authority (MPA) I regularly joined with the Green member Jenny Jones (against the rest) in upholding the need to ensure fairness for demonstrators and other aspects of civil liberties which need to be kept at the forefront of policing oversight, however unpopular it makes you with the establishment. And I joined the awkward squad Equalities and Diversities Committee where the Tories simply blanked it. We certainly were not Tories in mourning."

Hockney, whatever we may care to say about his politics, does conjure up some fascinating possibilities for UKIP. He concludes, "If the 'racist/BNP in blazers' argument relating to the current heavy reliance upon immigration can be buried or put into a form of proportion, it might even be quite attractive for progressives to have a 'bunch of right wingers' elected demanding re-nationalisation, the removal of the NHS from the EU-US trade deal, and calling for Edward Snowden to be given asylum in the UK... Lord Owen was canny to try and coax UKIP on the NHS issue. This one will at some point take root if policy is seriously given priority. Others might usefully try the same and lobby UKIP on aspects of policy about which they feel strongly."

It's almost irrelevant discussing the sincerity or otherwise of those who would re-brand and market UKIP as a worker-friendly vehicle. As is often the case in politics perception is reality and Labour's capitulation to the market and austerity leaves it wide open to attacks from the left. That UKIP, of all parties, should attempt such an attack is almost admirable in its audacity.

The fact remains that irrespective of its dismissal as loonies, racists and more unhinged Tories, UKIP is attracting support from sectors that Labour once could — indeed, did — take for granted. However amusing some may find Farage's shameless and opportunistic parking of UKIP tanks on Labour's lawn, albeit lawns Labour long since abandoned, one doubts that Ed Miliband is among their number.

Chapter 9: ...
and Then a Step
to the Ri·i·ight

"The Second World Wide War was engineered by the Zionist Jews"
Former UKIP East Sussex Council candidate
Anna-Marie Crampton.

That UKIP is a threat to Labour's vote almost as much as it is to that of the Tories is something the *Telegraph's* Damian Thompson recognises. In an article from March, 2014, he, too, almost presents UKIP as a left-of-centre-leaning party, which merely needs to weed out its non-representative racists and bigots. Of course Thompson is far too canny an operator to explicitly offer such a ridiculous premise but he certainly comes close: "I had coffee with Peter Whittle this week. He's an openly gay British writer and former television executive who spent years working in Los Angeles. He founded and runs a trendy think tank called the New Culture Forum (NCF). He is unequivocally anti-racist and supports gay marriage. Also, he's just been made the culture spokesman for the United Kingdom Independence Party."

Well, there you go. UKIP's snagged one of them there cosmopolitan, middle-class, anti-racist, pro-gay types. Don't worry, socialists; UKIP's got this covered. You can go home now. Game over.

As well as opening a column with one of the most patronising paragraphs in recent tabloid journalism, Thompson goes on to stretch the UKIP-as-proletarian-vanguardists concept to the sort of lengths that only Salvador Dali could have imagined. Thompson's thesis is that people one might not normally associate with UKIP are now attracted to the party because of its opposition to "multiculturalism and its weaselly contempt for Britain" with Whittle being a prime example.

Whittle heads up the New Culture Forum (NCF) and his UKIP membership has Thompson squealing with delight: "I didn't know Whittle was a member of Ukip. What a smart appointment by Nigel Farage! The NCF is my favourite think tank."

The NCF declares its mission statement thus:

> In the last quarter of the 20th century, the Right decisively won the important economic arguments. But in the so-called Culture Wars, the liberal Left have dominated.
>
> The triumph of cultural relativism and political correctness in the opinion-forming fields of the media, academia, education and culture has meant that these attitudes have become even more deeply entrenched. What started out as a counter-culture has become the reigning orthodoxy.
>
> With the recent movement of the political right towards the so-called 'centre ground', even fewer dissenting voices are heard. The liberal establishment sets the terms of debate.
>
> At a time of threat from extremism, the West finds itself besieged from within and without. Too often our enemies and our opinion formers appear to agree that Western culture is an indefensible horror. This is nonsense. The West is in fact a unique bastion of reasoned freedom. Britain in particular should be proud of the great role it has played in Western education, art and culture.
>
> We formed the New Culture Forum as a response to this situation. An association of people who work in the media and cultural arenas, the NCF is the first body of its kind to draw specifically on these areas.

It's difficult to see why Whittle's UKIP membership so excites Thompson. The above world-view meshes perfectly with UKIP orthodoxy. Indeed, although slightly better-written, it could easily pass for a *Daily Mail* editorial.

Apparently it's because, "Peter Whittle is someone who could persuade middle-of-the-road voters to support Ukip. His appointment is a reminder that Nigel Farage can be nuanced and flexible when it suits him — note how skilfully (i.e. unobtrusively) he ditched Ukip's campaign against gay marriage this week on the grounds that the battle is lost."

Thompson quotes Whittle explaining his thinking: "We must replace multiculturalism with integration. Britain must be totally colour-blind but reject any subtle ambivalence about national pride" Before concluding his column with an appeal to Farage: "This isn't to say that Nigel Farage is wrong to chase the protest vote, or that he should tone down his attacks on the corruption of Brussels and the Conservatives' terrified cringing in the face of Left-wing pressure groups. But he's got to stop giving 'maverick' activists the benefit of the doubt when, as happened recently, one of them talks about 'sending them all back' — and he has to find a way to drown out the professional bores who bang on about 'LibLabCon traitors' in online discussion forums. They're hijacking your brand, Nigel, and driving away potential supporters just when you should be entering the mainstream."

So there you have it. UKIP is a "mainstream" political outfit unfortunately victim to racists, nutters and cranks intent on "hijacking" the party.

The Independent was even more explicit on January 2nd, 2015, when it reported that "Ukip is preparing to roll out a series of populist policies to woo Labour voters in the run up to the general election and move the party away from its traditional right-wing roots." The paper accurately predicted that Farage would roll out a number of prole-friendly measures which would include "ring-fencing the National Health Service budget, raising the income tax threshold for lower earners and opposing a new runway at Heathrow." All, of course, with the intention of changing people's perception that UKIP is simply the Tory id unchained with the aim of widening support amongst the traditional working class.

The Independent continued, "Recent polls have put Ukip's national support at between 12 and 16 per cent.

But party strategists have long believed they have maximised their support from the right — and need to look to the left for further gains."

A party spokesperson revealed to the newspaper that it was "... looking at the world as it is — and not how we might like it to be."

There can be little doubt that such moves are camouflage, or at least shameless vote-chasing with no regard for political integrity, rather than any genuine conversion to the cause of the working-class.

As the reader knows, there has been no definitive statement of the party's positions on a whole raft of policy issues and the 2015 general election manifesto is yet to surface.

Fortunately, for the interested potential UKIP voter, and as the reader will have noticed, its spokespeople aren't given to shyness or reticence regarding the key issues of the day. Sadly, however much its people reveal UKIP thinking, they can't generally be regarded as a reliable guide to UKIP policy. Or at least that's what Nigel Farage would have us believe. For every reality-free observation a UKIP representative makes regarding, say, homosexuals, the weather, Muslims, or immigrants, there usually follows a hasty addendum from Nigel laughing off such missteps as eccentricities or endearingly quaint individual foibles that are not representative of UKIP as a whole. There are those who suggest that such people reveal the *real* thinking of the average UKIPer and that Farage's glib denials are merely spin to keep the more sensitive — which is to say the less reactionary, racist and bigoted — voter on board. But that would be a bit cynical, no?

In any event, it leaves the would-be UKIP voter with something of a dilemma. How to know for what, exactly, one is voting where Farage and co are concerned?

Happily, finding policy detail isn't the frustratingly fruitless search for the UKIP Holy Grail that it once was. There is now at least some sort of measure by which

UKIP's commitment to the working-class can be measured.

Following the UKIP annual conference, held at Doncaster in the autumn of 2014 (where it encountered stiff opposition and picketing from local trade unions and assorted community organisations) it updated its website to include a more detailed overview of the policies we can expect to see form the spine of its election manifesto. Under the heading Policies for People we read:

> *The following statements represent highlights of UKIP's policy announcements as made at the Doncaster Conference. More detailed announcements will be made in the run up to the 2015 General Election.*

WHAT A UKIP GOVERNMENT WILL DO

Protecting jobs and increasing prosperity

- *We would review all legislation and regulations from the EU (3,600 new laws since 2010) and remove those which hamper British prosperity and competitiveness.*

- *We would negotiate a bespoke trade agreement with the EU to enable our businesses to continue trading to mutual advantage.*

- *UKIP would not seek to remain in the European Free Trade Area (EFTA) or European Economic Area (EEA) while those treaties maintain a principle of free movement of labour, which prevents the UK managing its own borders.*

- *We would reoccupy the UK's vacant seat at the World Trade Organisation, ensuring that we continue to enjoy 'most favoured nation' status in trade with the EU, as is required under WTO rules.*

Repairing the UK Economy

- *UKIP will increase personal allowance to the level of full-time minimum wage earnings (approx £13,500 by next election).*

- *Inheritance tax will be abolished.*

- *We will introduce a 35p income tax rate between £42,285 and £55,000, whereupon the 40p rate becomes payable.*

- *UKIP will set up a Treasury Commission to design a turnover tax to ensure big businesses pay a minimum floor rate of tax as a proportion of their UK turnover.*

Reducing debts we leave to our grandchildren

- *UKIP will leave the EU and save at least £8bn pa in net contributions.*

- *UKIP will cut the foreign aid budget by £9bn pa, prioritising disaster relief and schemes which provide water and inoculation against preventable diseases.*

- *UKIP will scrap the HS2 project which is uneconomical and unjustified.*

- *UKIP will abolish the Department of Energy and Climate Change and scrap green subsidies.*

- *UKIP will abolish the Department for Culture Media and Sport.*

- *UKIP will reduce Barnett Formula spending and give devolved parliaments and assemblies further tax powers to compensate.*

Prioritising Education and Skills

- *UKIP will introduce an option for students to take an Apprenticeship Qualification instead of four non-core GCSEs which can be continued at A-Level. Students can take up apprenticeships in jobs with certified professionals qualified to grade the progress of the student.*

- *Subject to academic performance UKIP will remove tuition fees for students taking approved degrees in science, medicine, technology, engineering, maths on the condition that they live, work and pay tax in the UK for five years after the completion of their degrees.*

- *UKIP will scrap the target of 50% of school leavers going to university.*

- *Students from the EU will pay the same student fee rates as International students.*

- *UKIP supports the principle of Free Schools that are open to the whole community and uphold British values.*

- *Existing schools will be allowed to apply to become grammar schools and select according to ability and* aptitude. Selection ages will be flexible and determined by the school in consultation with the local authority.

- Schools will be investigated by OFSTED on the presentation of a petition to the Department for Education signed by 25% of parents or governors.

Honouring the Military Covenant

- We will resource fully our military assets and personnel.
- UKIP will guarantee those who have served in the Armed Forces for a minimum of 12 years a job in the police force, prison service or border force.
- UKIP will change the points system for social housing to give priority to ex-service men and women and those returning from active service.
- A Veterans Department will bring together all veterans services to ensure servicemen and women get the after-service care they deserve.
- Veterans are to receive a Veterans' Service Card to ensure they are fast tracked for mental health care and services, if needed.
- All entitlements will be extended to servicemen recruited from overseas.
- UKIP supports a National Service Medal for all those who have served in the armed forces.

The National Health Service

- UKIP will ensure the NHS is free at the point of delivery and time of need for all UK residents.
- We will stop further use of PFI in the NHS and encourage local authorities to buy out their PFI contracts early where this is affordable.
- We will ensure that GPs' surgeries are open at least one evening per week, where there is demand for it.
- UKIP opposes plans to charge patients for visiting their GP.
- We will ensure that visitors to the UK, and migrants until they have paid NI for five years, have NHS-approved private health insurance as a condition of entry to the UK, saving the NHS £2bn pa. UKIP will commit to spending £200m of the £2bn saving to end hospital car parking charges in England.

- We will replace Monitor and the Care Quality Commission with elected county health boards to be more responsive scrutineers of local health services. These will be able to inspect health services and take evidence from whistle-blowers.

- UKIP opposes the sale of NHS data to third parties.

- We will ensure foreign health service professionals coming to work in the NHS are properly qualified and can speak English to a standard acceptable to the profession.

- UKIP will amend working time rules to give trainee doctors, surgeons and medics the proper environment to train and practise.

- There will be a duty on all health service staff to report low standards of care.

Controlling and managing our borders

- UKIP recognises the benefits of limited, controlled immigration.

- UKIP will leave the EU, and take back control of our borders. Work permits will be permitted to fill skills gaps in the UK jobs market.

- We will extend to EU citizens the existing points-based system for time-limited work permits. Those coming to work in the UK must have a job to go to, must speak English, must have accommodation agreed prior to their arrival, and must have NHS-approved health insurance.

- Migrants will only be eligible for benefits (in work or out of work) when they have been paying tax and NI for five years and will only be eligible for permanent residence after ten years.

- UKIP will reinstate the primary purpose rule for bringing foreign spouses and children to the UK.

- UKIP will not offer an amnesty for illegal immigrants or those gaining British passports through fraud.

- UKIP will return to the principles of the UN Convention of Refugees which serves to protect the most vulnerable.

Foreign Aid

- UKIP will target foreign aid at healthcare initiatives, inoculations against preventable diseases and clean water

*programmes with a much-reduced aid budget adminis-
tered by the Foreign Office.*

- *British organisations will be offered the contracts to deliver
the remaining aid following removal of the EU
Procurement Directive.*

Energy

- *UKIP will repeal the Climate Change Act 2008 which costs
the economy £18bn a year.*

- *UKIP supports a diverse energy market including coal,
nuclear, shale gas, geo-thermal, tidal, solar, conventional
gas and oil.*

- *We will scrap the Large Combustion Plant Directive and
encourage the re-development of British power stations, as
well as industrial units providing on-site power generation.*

- *UKIP supports the development of shale gas with proper
safeguards for the local environment. Community
Improvement Levy money from the development of shale
gas fields will be earmarked for lower council taxes or community projects within the local authority being developed.*

- *There will be no new subsidies for wind farms and solar
arrays.*

- *UKIP will abolish green taxes and charges in order to
reduce fuel bills.*

Agriculture and Fishing

- *By leaving the EU, the UK will leave the Common Agri-
cultural Policy. Outside the EU UKIP will institute a British
Single Farm Payment for farms.*

- *UKIP will let the British parliament vote on GM foods.*

- *UKIP will leave the Common Fisheries Policy and reinstate
British territorial waters.*

- *Foreign trawlers would have to apply for and purchase
fishing permits to fish British waters when fish stocks have
returned to sustainable levels.*

- *Food must be labelled to include the country of origin,
method of production, method of slaughter, hormones
and any genetic additives.*

- *UKIP will abolish the export of live animals for slaughter.*

133

Welfare and Childcare

- UKIP opposes the bedroom tax because it operates unfairly, penalising those who are unable to find alternative accommodation and taking insufficient account of the needs of families and the disabled.

- Child benefit is only to be paid to children permanently resident in the UK and future child benefit to be limited to the first two children only.

- UKIP will ensure there is an initial presumption of 50/50 shared parenting in child custody matters and grandparents will be given visitation rights.

- UKIP supports a simplified, streamlined welfare system and a benefit cap.

Transport

- We will scrap HS2.

- UKIP opposes tolls on public roads and will let existing contracts for running toll roads expire.

- UKIP will maintain pensioner bus passes.

- UKIP will require foreign vehicles to purchase a Britdisc, before entry to the UK, in order to contribute to the upkeep of UK roads and any lost fuel duty.

- UKIP will ensure that speed cameras are used as a deterrent and not as a revenue raiser for local authorities.

Housing and planning

- UKIP will protect the Green Belt.

- Planning rules in the NPPF will be changed to make it easier to build on brownfield sites instead of greenfield sites. Central government is to list the nationally available brownfield sites for development and issue low-interest bonds to enable decontamination.

- Houses on brownfield sites will be exempt from Stamp Duty on first sale and VAT relaxed for redevelopment of brownfield sites.

- Planning Permission for large-scale developments can be overturned by a referendum triggered by the signatures of 5% of the District or Borough electors collected within three months.

Democracy and the Constitution

- UKIP will overcome the unfairness of MPs from devolved nations voting on English-only issues.

- UKIP supports the recall of MPs as was originally promised in the Coalition Agreement, whereby 20% of the electorate in a constituency must sign a recall petition within eight weeks. The approval of MPs will not be required to initiate a recall petition.

- UKIP will introduce the Citizens' Initiative to allow the public to initiate national referendums on issues of major public interest.

Law and Order

- UKIP will withdraw from the jurisdiction of the European Court of Human Rights.

- UKIP will reverse the government's opt-in to EU law and justice measures, including the European Arrest Warrant and European Investigation Order. We will replace the EAW with appropriate bi-lateral agreements.

- UKIP will not give prisoners the vote.

- UKIP believes that full sentences should be served and this should be taken into account when criminals are convicted and sentenced in court. Parole should be available for good behaviour on a case-by-case basis, not systematically.

- We will repeal the Human Rights Act and replace it with a new British Bill of Rights. The interests of law-abiding citizens & victims will always take precedence over those of criminals.

Culture

- UKIP recognises and values an overarching, unifying British culture, which is open and inclusive to anyone who wishes to identify with Britain and British values, regardless of their ethnic or religious background.

- Official documents will be published in English and, where appropriate Welsh and Scots Gaelic.

- UKIP will ensure that the law is rigorously enforced in relation to 'cultural' practices which are illegal in Britain, such as forced marriages, FGM and so-called 'honour killings'

- *We will review the BBC Licence Fee with a view to its reduction. Prosecution of non-payments of the Licence Fee would be taken out of the criminal sphere and made a civil offence.*

- *UKIP will amend the smoking ban to give pubs and clubs the choice to open smoking rooms properly ventilated and separated from non-smoking areas.*

- *UKIP opposes 'plain paper packaging' for tobacco products and minimum pricing of alcohol.*

Employment and Small Businesses

- *Businesses should be able to discriminate in favour of young British workers.*

- *Repeal the Agency Workers Directive.*

- *Conduct a skills review to better inform our education system and qualifications*

- *Encourage councils to provide more free parking for the high street.*

- *Simplify planning regulations and licences for empty commercial property vacant for over a year.*

- *Extend the right of appeal for micro businesses against HMRC action.*

The above is quite an astonishing pick 'n' mix amalgam of centre-right populism, opportunist bolt-on gestures to Labour voters and a fiercely pro-business right-wing libertarianism — allowing the market as much of a free reign as is practicably possible — anything that hinders the right of business to make profit must be removed. UKIP sees the EU as the evil preventing the flourishing of the British economy.

Sadly, for the would-be UKIP member who has to work for a living in a normal job, rather than dining on the tax payer's largesse, not a word is to be found on wages, employment protection or workplace rights. Business comes first, last and always.

As well as making a virtue of a disregard for the environment, the most notable aspect of the party's thinking in the relevant areas is the number of jobs UKIP is cheerfully prepared to see shed as a result of a further reduction of the public sector by the abolition of entire departments. The rest is a disturbing mix of the hilarious and terrifying. Ex-soldiers, trained killers, to be guaranteed civil enforcement roles with, seemingly, no concern for the dangers to public safety such a move might entail. Not a word on trade unions, the minimum wage, maternity leave or women but plenty of help for the party's tobacco baron pals. And, of course, barely a sentence on how any of the above would be funded and paid for.

On the question of the NHS, UKIP continues to bounce around all over the place. While it claims official policy is for a publicly-funded, free-at-the-point-of-use national health service, Farage is on record as supporting privatisation. *The Independent* reported in November, 2014, that he'd been secretly filmed telling supporters that "the NHS should move away from the state-funded model, and towards a US-style insurance-based system."

He would, it was claimed, be far more "comfortable" with the "marketplace" having access to British health provision. Perhaps he hasn't heard of PFI or has taken his eye off the Tory wrecking ball that's been careering through the NHS since 2010.

The video, claims *The Independent*, shows Farage saying "I think we are going to have to move to an insurance-based system of healthcare. Frankly, I would feel more comfortable that my money would return value if I was able to do that through the marketplace of an insurance company, than just us trustingly giving £100billion a year to central government and expecting them to organise the healthcare service from cradle to grave for us."

Obviously the opposition were quick to react with Andy Burnham first into attack when he told the *Guardian* "Nigel Farage poses as a man of the people, but his views on the NHS are out of step with 99% of the public. Farage can drink as many pints as he likes, but he'll never be able to distance himself from these views that would go down like a lead balloon in pubs and clubs across the land. It is now plain for all to see that a vote for Ukip is a vote for the privatisation of the NHS."

UKIP leaped into damage-limitation mode with a spokesperson claiming that, "Obviously things have moved on significantly since then. That was then and this is now. It doesn't stand up to say that's still his view" and that people in the party now know "significantly more about the NHS".

Mind you, it wasn't just Farage who appeared to favour completing New Labour's and the Tories Project Privatise NHS. His fellow MEP Paul Nuttall is on record heaping approval on the Conservatives for adding a "whiff of privatisation to the NHS".

Yet as recently as March 2015 Farage was back in the headlines for his remarks favouring that which his party had previously claimed to reject; the privatisation of the NHS.

In an interview with the BBC's Nick Robinson, Farage said, "I triggered a debate within Ukip that was outright rejected by my colleagues, so I have to accept that. As time goes on, this is a debate that we're all going to have to return to. There is no question that healthcare provision is going to have to be very much greater in 10 years than it is today, with an ageing population, and we're going to have to find ways to do it."

His remarks seemed to set him at odds with the rest of the party as Louise Blours, UKIP's Health Spokesperson, stated, "What people have to realise about Ukip is that we are much more democratic than other parties. Nigel is entitled to his opinion and others are entitled to theirs, we don't whip people into all thinking the same thing, like the establishment parties. As he has said before, he raised the idea for discussion a while ago, the party discussed at and rejected it. I am certain that if the party discuss it again, we will reject it again. The vast majority of Ukip members, the British public and I will always favour a state funded NHS."

Others remain unconvinced with Kailish Chande telling the *Guardian,* "Ukip is known for making its policy on the hoof. But it was Ukip that said the NHS was not fit for the 21st century. It was Ukip that promised to impose £40bn of cuts to our NHS; that it would franchise out key services including hospitals and GP surgeries to companies and charities. The party is in favour of charging patients who require A&E treatment, but who don't need treating within two hours, and it will promote mutual providers, including GPs, to charge a flat fee to see non-emergency cases. It also wants to make sure that when people register with a GP they can demonstrate that they will be able to pay off upfront fees over a period of time".

If there were doubts that Farage was no fan of the NHS, the publication of his latest autobiographical account of UKIP's rise to prominence offered its supporters a worryingly ambivalent picture. In *The Purple Revolution,* he writes about his experiences receiving treatment for testicular cancer: "to say that this consultant was disinterested would be an understatement; perhaps he had a round of golf booked for the afternoon. 'Keep taking the antibiotics,' he preached, and that was that.' I have now had three near-death experiences — cancer, an accident and a plane crash — and I've seen the best and worst of the NHS. I am better qualified to criticise and defend our health care system than most politicians. When I had cancer, the incompetence and negligence of the NHS almost killed me, but it has also saved my life. I am certainly not taking any flak from gutless politicians who claim that I am no fan or supporter of the NHS."

Several things are possible here; Farage, and UKIP policy-makers, could change the party's policy on the NHS, in a transparent attempt to woo Labour voters and/or it's an example of politicians saying what they really think in private and then saying something quite different in public. If you can imagine such a thing.

It's interesting to speculate that the NHS could prove to be the issue that does UKIP real internal damage. A split between Farage's unfettered free marketers and defecting Labour voters could easily occur if the party is placed under pressure.

Farage's bread landed butter side up when his plans to Labourise UKIP were handed a propaganda bonus by a high-profile Labour defection. "One of Labour's most senior figures has resigned from the party and will be supporting Ukip because of Ed Miliband's failure to offer a referendum on Britain's membership of the European Union," reported the *Telegraph* on February 17th, 2015.

Harriet Yeo, who'd previously enjoyed a stint as Chair of Labour's National Executive Committee was said to be so disgruntled by Miliband's refusal to support a referendum on Europe that she decided to throw in her lot with UKIP.

Yeo is a long-standing trade unionist, with twenty years-plus membership and then presidency of the Transport and Salaried Staffs' Association. One can imagine Farage's delight at landing such a fish as he seeks to win over Labour voters. We didn't need to imagine for long. The UKIP leader was chuffed, announcing, "I'm delighted that UKIP can now count upon the support of such respected figure as Harriet Yeo. A life long Trade Unionist and Labour Party member who served as Chair of Ed Miliband's NEC she is yet another voice calling for Britain to have a choice about its future. We are welcoming support from across the board and Harriet's support is evidence of this."

It seemed that it wasn't just Europe that had caused Yeo's departure. As the *Telegraph* reported, "Mrs Yeo has previously attacked the 'awful' culture inside her trade union and said she has witnessed 'outrageous' behaviour behind closed doors. She recounted how male colleagues deliberately organised a lap-dancing party to clash with a black-tie dinner that had been arranged by female union officials to celebrate 100 years of International Women's Day."

Of course the idea that such things wouldn't happen in UKIP, of all parties, is perhaps leaning towards naivety.

Labour hit back with gossip circulating that Yeo was taking her revenge for the party deselecting her. There were rumours of her poor attendance at various meetings and so she was characterised as someone making the best of a bad job while taking the chance to give her former party a bit of a kicking on the way out. A Labour insider was quoted by the *Telegraph* rubbishing Yeo's claims and said that "the vast majority of the Labour Party are united behind our position on Europe, believing Britain's best interests are served by staying in a reformed EU and not sleepwalking towards an exit which would cost British jobs and influence."

It needs to be pointed out, however, that such an occurrence says far, far more about Labour's gallop to the right than it does about UKIP's insincere and entirely cosmetic posturing to the left.

Nevertheless, it was a blow to Ed Miliband and a PR triumph for Nigel Farage. Providing a welcoming home for Labour defectors can do Farage's attempts to poach Labour's core vote no harm at all.

Chapter 10:
Je Suis Nigel?

"The idea that Nigel Farage is some sort of voice of the working class, frankly, is bollocks"
Labour MP for Barnsley East **Michael Dugher**

At the time of writing this chapter, political observers are studying events in Greece with great interest. In contrast to a resurgent far right mentioned earlier in this book, in Greece it's the far(ish) left that has captured the public mood with anti-austerity defiance. It's irrelevant to the point at hand that that defiance may well turn out to be little more than wafer-thin; it's the fact that Syriza managed to win state power on a program effectively the diametric opposite of that which UKIP espouses. Yet in the UK it's Farage's neo-Powellites that are tapping into the anger, confusion and resentment of large swathes of the disenfranchised, desperate and frightened. In the UK, no matter how desperately various components of the left declare themselves the English Syriza, the fact remains that they could barely fill a 'phone booth with their voters. UKIP, on the other hand...

By now no one with even the most casual relationship with reality could dispute that it's UKIP — not the left — dictating political discourse in England. The potential impact on Labour could be devastating. As journalist David Osler remarks in a piece for *Left Futures* from February 2015:

> Not a few superannuated Bennites, and indeed anybody who prefers their social democracy served straight no chaser, will be entirely entranced by Greek politics right now. Here, for the first time in three decades, is a left-wing European government locked into a collision course with neo-liberalism.

Circumstances specific to that country have enabled Syriza to win an election on a radical economic platform somewhere towards the outer limits of anything that could successfully be advanced anywhere in Europe. Indeed, some of the proposals put forward by its finance minister Yanis Varoufakis were drawn up with input from Stuart Holland, late of this parish and a key architect of the Alternative Economic Strategy once favoured by the Labour left.

Yet Syriza faces oppositional forces far greater than those that derailed the Mitterrand administration in France between 1981 and 1983, an experiment generally hailed as the last hurrah for the parliamentary road to socialism.

To update Marx, it is as if all the powers of old Europe have entered into a holy alliance to exorcise this spectre; central banker and bond trader, Schulz and Juncker, French prime ministers and German chancellors.

Anyone who believes that citizens have the right to decide their country's economic direction without facing a veto from finance capital will be hugely sympathetic to what Syriza is trying to pull off, whatever doubts they harbour as to its ability to achieve its stated goals. But some go further and contend that what is happening in Greece offers some sort of alternative prospectus for Britain.

The buzzword Pasokification — coined by Labour activist James Doran — has gained currency online as a prognosis for the future of Labour. It has even made it into The Guardian, while Michael Meacher has employed the term. As far as I know, a rigorous definition has yet to be established. But the basic connotation is clear enough; following Pasok's virtual wipe-out at the ballot box, the word is intended to describe sudden collapse of a previously dominant social democratic party, much in the manner of a jerry-built Bangladeshi textiles factory.

Some sections of the far left salivate palpably, in the belief that the Pasokification is both inevitable and desirable. The idea is that if only Labour would gulp down the single malt, clasp the pearl-handled revolver and do the decent thing, then a mass radical left formation would spring up to take its place.

Proponents of this thesis should be careful what they wish for. If Labour does succumb to Pasokification, there is no guarantee that Britain will Syriza-ise in consequence.

Of course it would be complacent to dismiss the disintegration scenario out of hand. That Labour is a hollow shell in many constituencies is beyond dispute. The situation is particularly acute in Scotland, thanks to a triple whammy of the

Falkirk imbroglio, the alliance with the Tories over the independence referendum and the branch office's subsequent 'crisis, what crisis?' reaction in plumping for a Blairite leader. Little wonder that the SNP is eating up the Labour vote north of the border.

In the rest of the country, the Greens are making headway among the Guardianistas and — horribly, unimaginably — UKIP's ugly rehashed Thatcherism on racist steroids is eroding chunks of what the Blairites sniggeringly designated by the euphemism of the 'heartland vote'.

Labour obviously has no any greater claim on immortality than any other sublunary phenomenon. Political parties evolve over time, as the long view of British history makes plain. What Labour will look like five or ten years from now is an open question. But it also needs to be stressed Labour is a qualitatively different entity from Pasok. Not the least of the distinctions is its far deeper roots in past mass movements in British society, stretching back to the Chartism of the nineteenth century.

Pasok, by contrast, is pretty much a one-man job, being the relatively recent creation of the late Andreas Papandreou, a scion of the Greek political elite who never knowingly let principle stand in the way of opportunity.

Launched at the restoration of democracy in Greece in 1974, it initially positioned itself as a national liberation movement, to the point of developing ties to Gaddafi's Libya and Ba'athist Syria. It did not gravitate towards the Socialist International mainstream until as late as 1980, the year prior to its first electoral victory and Greece's accession to the EU. Even at that time, its politics were marked by strident nationalism.

Nor has it ever been hegemonic in the Greek labour movement, with Greece's unabashedly Stalinist communist party KKE always the strongest ideological force in the trade unions. Pasok was, in short, a rather flimsier edifice than Labour, and if its existence proves more ephemeral, that can come as no great surprise.

Meanwhile, it is more likely than not that Ed Miliband will be Britain's next prime minister. At the very least, Labour will come out of May's general election with about 300 seats, give or take a few dozen either way. Talk of its impending death is has seemingly a greater basis in wishful thinking than in boring old reality.

Let's say Miliband loses and is ousted by the Progress tendency, which proceeds to deepen Labour's disconnect with a *public that has repeatedly made clear that it positively craves more social housing, railway nationalisation and a higher minimum wage. Even in that case, there is no evidence for the proposition that a Syriza-style alliance of the radical left would emerge as a credible formation in a country where Elvis impersonators routinely enjoy greater success than the sundry Trotskyist electoral vehicles.*

Syriza's culture, after all, is based on eurocommunism, a doctrine in which the idea of broad alliances with amenable sections of the right is central. Not even having to get into bed with ANEL was considered out of bounds by Syriza's majority.

By contrast, initiatives such TUSC are dominated by two groups have been at daggers drawn throughout their entire respective existences. This town ain't big enough for the both of the central committees. The greater likelihood is that a Pasokified Labour Party's electoral support would dissipate among the new contender mentioned above, with the bulk of union political funds continuing to go to whatever rebranded post-Labourite formation Mr Umunna or Ms Reeves find themselves heading.

As a result, British politics would see itself ratcheted permanently even further to the right of where it is now.

Without a meaningful Labour Party, Britain would face permanent rule by the Tories or by Tory-led coalitions, perhaps including UKIP. If you want a picture of the future, imagine a boot stamping on the face of a benefit claimant — forever.

Given the weather in Britain this February, daydreaming about a summer holiday spent knocking back chilled retsina in a Greek island taverna as bouzoukis chime in the background is a harmless enough indulgence. But just remember that a Greek transformation of British politics is a destination somewhat further away than anywhere to which aasyJet currently flies.

While the author feels Osler is a tad too breezy regarding Labour's electoral fortunes and short-to-medium term prospects, he is on the money where it counts; it is UKIP, not any formulation to Labour's left, that is gaining electoral momentum and attacking the Labour vote. Along with that of the Tories', of course.

If anyone is still wondering about the seeming emphasis on Labour, in a book about UKIP, then let me make it abundantly clear. This author, along with the readers —

I hope — has enjoyed many a chuckle at UKIP's expense over the preceding pages but the time for laughter is over. UKIP will take votes from the centre, right *and* left — insofar as that word still applies to Labour in any meaningful sense — and it's much too late to hope that Labour, British capitalism's second eleven, will do anything to seriously challenge the current consensus. That is completely ruled out.

The far left, too, in the guise of the Trade Union and Socialist Coalition or the Ken Loach-inspired Left Unity (of which the author is nominally a member) hasn't got a hope in hell, for different reasons, of making any kind of significant impact at the polls in May, 2015.

We are where we are because the Conservatives, Labour and Liberal Democrats are united in their acceptance of austerity and the supremacy of capital. Each, in its own way, tries to mark itself as different from the other two but the differences are purely cosmetic and concerned with degree, not ideology. In Labour's case, there is some added hand-wringing and a few crocodile tears but that's about your lot.

Paradoxically, it's the absence of an alternative that boosts support for a party like UKIP which offers no alternative and is even further to the right than the Conservatives. But it *looks* like an alternative and when people are desperate, they'll try anything.

Returning to Greece-UK comparisons, for a moment, Aditya Chakrabortty offered his analysis in a column for the *Guardian* on January, 27th, 2015: "... instead of speculating about Syriza's future, we should draw one vital lesson from its very recent past — one that Ed Miliband and his inner circle ought to learn too. Because there's no way that Alexis Tsipras would have been sworn in as prime minister had it not been for the disastrous and ultimately suicidal behaviour of Labour's sister party in Greece, Pasok. The death of the country's main centre-left organisation has been swift and spectacular." Chakrabortty goes further than Osler when considering

Labour's decline: "It would take a particular blindness to look at today's Labour party — home to the descendants of Kinnocks, Benns, Straws and Goulds, as well as a host of sleek former special advisers — and not see in it traces of the same toxic eliteness that killed Pasok. You can push the comparisons further. Labour rightly attacks the coalition for its economy-capsizing austerity, but then brings out its own programme of massive spending cuts. Pasok saw Greece's manufacturing base crumble; Labour waited until the crash to bang on about an industrial strategy. Pasok took its vote for granted; there are whole tranches of Britain where Labour assumes the electoral maths will work its way forever."

He concludes in grimly prophetic style: "Over the past few years, Syriza's thinkers have sometimes quoted a text as a kind of description of their window of opportunity. It is from Antonio Gramsci's *Prison Notebooks*. In it, the Italian communist notes: 'At a certain point in their historical lives, social classes become detached from their traditional parties ... The particular men who constitute, represent, and lead them, are no longer recognised by their class (or fraction of a class) as its expression.' That applies to Greece, yes. But tell me it is not also true of Britain."

So that's Labour. What of the Tories? A depressing example of their equally shameless attempts to usurp UKIP saw the party, on February, 17th, 2015, take UKIP's policy regarding the unemployed and give it that typically nasty Tory spin. Cameron announced plans to make benefits claimants work thirty hours a week for their dole money. Lizzie Dearden, of *The Independent*, reported: "David Cameron's plan to force young people to work for benefits would see them working 30 hours a week for a fraction of the minimum wage, it emerged today. The proposals would put young adults who have been out of work, education or training for six months ("neets") into compulsory community work such as making meals for the elderly or joining local charities.

Under the scheme, Jobseekers' Allowance would be abolished for 18 to 21-year-olds and replaced with the already announced 'Youth Allowance' of the same amount — £57.35 a week, or £1.91 per hour of work."

Cameron claims his party's measures would "effectively abolish long-term youth unemployment" and that they "are not just about saving money. They are about changing lives and making this a country that rewards work and gives everyone the chance of a better future. That is why we are taking further steps to help young people make something of their lives. Our goal in the next parliament is effectively to abolish long-term youth unemployment. We want to get rid of that well-worn path from the school gate, down to the Jobcentre, and on to a life on benefits."

Ah, yes, that well-known anti-working class myth, beloved of Tory and Labour minister alike, that of the feckless proles, who leave school and content themselves with a life on the dole. Not least the Joseph Rowntree Foundation has shown such received wisdom to be nonsense. Along with that equally well-worn Tory favourite, the family where no one has worked for umpteen generations.

Cameron had the neck to lecture that working class youth need "work experience and the order and discipline of turning up for work each day." It's obvious to anyone that such "order and discipline" might best be acquired by actually having a job to do. In the absence of one, then, Cameron and co are happy to kick the unemployed and blame them for the failure of British capitalism to provide sufficient employment for the UK's unemployed young.

"From day one they must realise that welfare is not a one-way street. Yes, we will help them, but there is no more something for nothing. They must give back to their community too." Working for less than the legal minimum wage, then. Working for dole money. Slave labour by any other name. And right on cue, here's the Labour leader frantically doing his me-too thing as the article concluded, "Ed Miliband has also warned that young unemployed people who refuse to comply with the scheme could lose benefits under a Labour government."

Marx was depressingly accurate when he observed that "The ideas of the ruling class are in every epoch the ruling ideas, i.e. the class which is the ruling material force of society, is at the same time its ruling intellectual force."

For decades the ideological terrain has been shifting in favour of a party like UKIP and we're now in an era where facts have never been as worthless as they are today. Instead, an entirely false perception exists regarding the kind of Britain in which we currently live.

A 2013 poll by Ipsos Mori showed exactly how warped things have become when its research revealed just how wide of the mark the average Brit is regarding key questions of the period.

The public believed that £24 of every £100 of benefits were fraudulently claimed. In reality, just seventy pence in every £100 is fraudulently claimed.

On immigration, those questioned believed that 31 per cent of the recent population growth consisted of immigrants. The reality was 13 percent. Even when including illegal immigrants, the true figure struggled to reach 15 per cent. Similarly, on questions of race and ethnicity black and Asian people were believed to comprise over thirty percent of the population when the figure barely scraped into 11 percent.

On the matter of Godfrey Bloom's Bongo Bongo land, the public thought that around 26 percent of GDP went on foreign aid. In truth, it was 1.1 percent. They also believed it was one of the top three items of state expenditure.

Back to benefits and the sample revealed 29 percent of people believed that more money is allocated to Job Seekers' Allowance than pensions when more than fifteen times is spent on pensions than unemployment benefit: £4.9 billion on benefits compared to nearly £75 billion on pensions.

A Royal Statistical Society spokesperson said that "Our data poses real challenges for policymakers. How can you develop good policy when public perceptions can be so out of kilter with the evidence?" Indeed. "We need to see three things happen. First, politicians need to be better at talking about the real state of affairs of the country, rather than spinning the numbers. Secondly, the media has to try and genuinely illuminate issues, rather than use statistics to sensationalise." And we can say neither of those things is ever going to happen.

An Ipsos Mori representative hinted at something nearer reality: "A lack of trust in government information is also very evident in other questions in the survey — so 'myth-busting' is likely to prove a challenge on many of these issues. But it is still useful to understand where people get their facts most wrong."

Things are even worse today with a political climate shaped by so much myth, prejudice and propaganda that UKIP can only feel confident as we head towards the next general election.

Two recent developments captured in bleak form the zeitgeist. The first of these was the latest furore around Top Gear's Jeremy Clarkson. The controversial presenter was involved in what was described as a 'fracas' when, at the end of a day's shooting, he returned to his hotel to find only cold buffet food available, instead of his preferred steak and chips. It was then alleged that he lost his temper with a producer, calling him an "incompetent, lazy Irish cunt" before launching a punch which may or may not have connected. Allegedly...

The incident is unremarkable; few would be surprised to imagine Clarkson behaving in such a manner. What was truly instructive was the public's reaction to the incident and to the BBC's handling thereof.

The BBC immediately suspended the presenter, pending an investigation, and offered no confirmation or denial regarding the allegations. No one else involved in the matter offered any comment, either. All quite correct and proper, one might feel. Well, it quickly became apparent that a significant chunk of the public felt quite differently as, by March 19th, 2015, a petition demanding his reinstatement edged towards one million.

What are we to make of such a development? That nearly a million people think punching a colleague at work is acceptable? Well, not quite. The comments on various social media platforms cleared the matter up. It became glaringly apparent that, given Clarkson's previous controversies regarding racist and/or bigoted comments, people felt he'd been a victim of political correctness!

And there we see the realisation of one of the greatest myths of the last thirty years; that we're ruled by so-called PC Police. That freedom of speech and the good old British way of life is under greater threat than it was when facing the Nazis in WWII. The reality is quite simply that most of Clarkson's supporters weren't even remotely outraged at the treatment of their hero. They were actually *delighted* because it provided them, they think, with some sort of twisted justification for their own pre-existing racism.

They welcomed the opportunity to rail against 'political correctness', to complain that things have gone too far in one direction and that there should now be an immediate return to the days before liberal meddlers and their political correctness ruined society, opened the flood gates and made it so as a decent white man can't even speak his mind in his own country any more. You know; a return to the gloried age when sooties didn't have chips on their shoulders and could take a joke. To the days when the Black and White Minstrel Show and Jim Davidson were just wholesome family entertainment and hotels proudly displayed signs proclaiming, 'No Dogs, No Blacks, No Irish'.

We live in an age when entirely untrue myths, deliberate lies and non-existent fantasies revolving around Christmas trees banned in the workplace, England football shirts banned from pubs and fast food outlets cowering in the face of Jihadist psychopaths, withdrawing pork from their menus are routinely accepted as fact. Such myths are blamed on political correctness which prevents freedom of speech. Or, in reality, simply reminds privileged, rich, white men that those unfortunate enough not to be male, white, rich and straight have feelings and rights too.

This is a climate which could not be more suited to UKIP. Something Paul Nuttall evidently recognises. In a 2015 article addressed to his supporters, UKIP's Deputy Chief took the myth of draconian political correctness and dragged it into the territory of tinfoil-hatted conspiracy theorists, while doing an admirable job of inventing some completely new fallacies.

Headed *Time for a Revolution Against the Marxists*, his article read:

Political correctness drives most of us mad — but how on earth did we end up like this in the first place?

In October 1917, Marxist Vladimir Lenin overthrew the Russian government heralding the beginning of seventy years of communism.

Many felt that the revolution would spread to Western Europe to countries such as France and Germany. Thank God it didn't.

In 1923 a group of depressed Marxist intellectuals gathered at Frankfurt am Main University in Germany to discuss the reasons why communism had not spread. They concluded that they had to change the way people thought and communicated before Western society was ready for it. They called this 'Cultural Marxism.'

This theory demanded that sympathisers indoctrinated the public by infiltrating the cultural institutions, including the media and universities.

When Hitler and the Nazis came to power in 1933, this group of Marxist academics, by then known as the Frankfurt School, fled Germany and settled in the United States.

And it was there where they were able to put their theory into practice. The 1960s Cultural Revolution gave the Marxists the perfect vehicle to experiment with their theory.

They clung to the coat-tails of the civil rights movement and cleverly stoked the anti-Vietnam War fire, even coining the famous phrase 'Make Love, Not War.'

> *Cultural Marxism became popular on student campuses in the United States in the late sixties and as with everything it spread to Britain.*
>
> *These days we know Cultural Marxism as 'political correctness.' The same political correctness that prevented police from doing anything about Pakistani men using underage girls in Rotherham as sex slaves.*
>
> *That ensures that in some prisons inmates are referred to as 'service users.' That says we shouldn't mention 'Christmas' in case it offends other faiths. The one used by far left loons to call you a racist if you want to protect our borders, or a homophobe if you think that homosexuality should not be taught to five year olds in schools.*
>
> *And it's the same political correctness that has given us so many second-rate political through enforced women-only shortlists and the 'I know my rights' society.*
>
> *It ensures that we don't complain when we're given Halal meat through fear of being called an Islamophobe, or frisked at an airport like a suspected terrorist, even though it's bloody obvious that you're not.*
>
> *The Cultural Marxists are winning. Over the past thirty years they have changed the way we speak and the way we think. They've made the downright nonsensical acceptable or politically incorrect.*
>
> *We've got to fight back. We have to say enough is enough and that the sexual abuse of 1,400 girls in Rotherham should be the last straw.*
>
> *I want to see a revolution in this country — a common sense revolution where we begin to say 'no thanks' to the Cultural Marxist politically correct mind benders.*

Such thinking is wide-spread. Fevered paranoia, downright historical untruths and evidence-free conjecture and speculation are now the accepted wisdom, all the while working in a few of those urban myths. Welcome to UKIP world.

If there is hope, it lies where? Revolution is looking somewhat unlikely. With the Greens? Some new formulation? No one would suggest for a moment that UKIP will win a general election. Such a prospect is impossible. But there is no need to. UKIP doesn't even need to be in government to shape government policy. They just have to exist.

Despite some commentators believing that UKIP has peaked, the *Guardian's* Suzanne Moore among them, such thinking is likely to be a case of premature celebration. Even with Farage's statement that should he not win his Thanet seat he'll resign as UKIP leader, UKIP is far from over. At least in the short-to-mid term — the long term of British politics is too grisly to even contemplate — they're here to stay. They aren't going away and both Labour and the Conservatives will continue making plans for Nigel.

Acknowledgements

As usual it's been a blast. Also as usual I've found the help and contributions of others invaluable.

Let me first thank my good friend Mick Wall for coming up with the concept and the title of the book in the first place. Cheers, brother. There would have been no book without Mick. You can send him hate-mail for this heinous act via www.mickwall.com

Thanks must go to Martin Rowson for an absolutely superb cover. Thank you so much for taking the job on, Martin.

My auld man, James Stewart Paterson for his steadfast support, interest and our typically combative political debates which helped sharpen some of the points in the book. David Osler, a good mate and a really great writer. Thanks, fella. Ross Bradshaw, my publisher, of Five Leaves who felt *Making Plans for Nigel* was worth a punt. Always a pleasure, pal. My wife Susan who, given this book was written under the most mental deadline I've ever encountered, was virtually a single woman for six weeks. Something she, oddly, seemed to take to quite well. Hmmm... Neil Cross, a dear friend, who read parts of the manuscript and offered honest and valuable advice.

Adam, Katy, Lorna and James all of whom, in their respective ways, made their support known.

And finally to the many friends who have been unfailingly supportive of this project. Far too many to mention all by name so please forgive me if you've been omitted. They include: Darren Patterson, Vick E Morris, Andrew Hawnt, Joel McIver, Mick Connole, Lisa McKenzie, Stewart Osborne, Floyd Codlin, Vinnie Turner, Abu-Tayeb KhairDeen, Phil Meynell, Paul Swift, Matt Hill, Phil Burton-Cartledge, Chech Lord, Martin Short, Russ Saxton, Paul Field, Sean Larkin, Stewart Henderson, Steve Glass, Annie Sands, Andy Foss, David Bell, Ruth Harris, Dale Deacon, Nicki Jameson, Mark Howard, Ian Mansell, Rick Palin, Martin Short.